W.D. GANN

DIVINATION BY MATHEMATICS

W.D. GANN

DIVINATION BY MATHEMATICS

AWODELE

UNION, KY

BEKH, LLC
UNION, KY
BEKHLLC@outlook.com

COPYRIGHT © 2013 BEKH, LLC
All rights reserved.

ISBN-13: 978-0615833439

TABLE OF CONTENTS

	PAGE
INTRODUCTION	7

CHAPTER

1   W.D. GANN   11
For those readers who may not know who W.D. Gann is, this chapter provides a little background information, some of his accomplishments, and why I believe his work is so important.

2   THE 1919 ARTICLE   13
The main goal of this book is the analysis of a little known article that Gann contributed to in 1919 in which he makes predictions concerning the German Kaiser, Wilhelm Hohenzollern. For the reader who is unfamiliar with this article, this chapter will familiarize the reader with its contents to prepare for its analysis in future chapters.

3   THE SCIENCE OF LETTERS & NUMBERS   21
This chapter introduces the reader to the system of letters and numbers that I believe Gann utilized in the 1919 article and the clue that led me to the evidence for this claim.

4   THE ASO-NEITH CRYPTOGRAM   26
This chapter provides details on the system of letters and number that I believe Gann utilizes in the 1919 article. Once we know what it is, we can learn how to use it, and will be better able to understand Gann's comments in the 1919 article.

5   CHARACTER ANALYSIS   55
This chapter focuses on how to perform character analysis using the system described in the previous chapter and then takes a look at how W.D. Gann may have used the same method in the 1919 article.

6   FORECASTING PER THE ASO-NEITH SYSTEM   **65**

This chapter focuses on how to forecast using the system described in the 4th chapter with the goal of ascertaining whether or not Gann used the same techniques to come up with the dates and periods that he forecasted in the 1919 article.

7   PERIODICITY   **70**

Continuing with the theme of the previous chapter, this chapter continues with ascertaining how Gann calculates the dates and periods that he forecasts in the 1919 article. However, it focuses on forecasting with respect to the periodic law, or law of octaves. This naturally leads into an analysis of cycles as well.

8   THE SECRET OF THE LAW OF VIBRATION   **93**

The final chapter concentrates on a section within the 1919 article in which Gann describes the process used to calculate a key number that he states would govern a person throughout their life. In the article, Gann tells us the key number for Woodrow Wilson and the components he used to calculate the key number. Since we have the ability to obtain these components for Woodrow Wilson, it allows us to see if we can decipher how Gann may have calculated the key number. As the article implies, the key number is the whole secret behind Mr. Gann's discovery.

BIBLIOGRAPHY   **101**

Introduction

In February of 1997 during my senior year of college, I was beginning a period of being exposed to wonderful ideas and concepts related to spirituality. I met who I would call my second and most influential spiritual teacher during this month. My good friend took me to see him for the first time in his office on campus during one of my breaks from classes. On the first visit he divined for me using an oracle system, performed a numerology reading based on my date of birth, and told me things about myself that were quite astonishing considering that this was the first time that we had ever met. I was fascinated and it sealed a friendship that has lasted to this day.

During the remaining part of my senior year and during graduate school I would continue to go by his office to visit, and he would always pass along books, notes, and material that he had picked up along the way to see if I resonated with the any of the information. Needless to say, I loved it all, but I will never forget the document he gave me with the title "Spiritual Development" written at the top. It was a copy of some handwritten notes dated November 2, 1975. There was no mention of the lecturer's name from which the notes were taken, but more importantly, the subject matter stimulated me like nothing else had before. I was captivated. The main theme of the notes dealt with cycles, and how the sages would learn to live in harmony with natural cycles and how to use them to his or her advantage. This lit an inner fire in me to learn as much about cycles as I could.

W.D. GANN: DIVINATION BY MATHEMATICS

As my interest and study of cycles grew, I obtained my first book on astrology during this time. Although this first book was on Vedic astrology, I have studied many forms of astrology over the years. Naturally, studying subjects such as cycles and astrology, I eventually came across the work of W.D. Gann. The first material I ever came across about Gann had nothing to do with the stock market or astrology. From what I remember, it just talked about Gann's concept of cycles and how he divided periods into their harmonic components. At the time, this is as far as I had delved into the work of Mr. W.D. Gann. However, as time passed I started to delve into stock market astrology and naturally Gann's name came up again. It was at this time that I realized how important his work was. Here we have an individual that could forecast the movement of stocks months and years in advance, and his ability to do so was well documented. After reading more about him and his work, I was intrigued, and set out to learn as much as I could.

Unfortunately, as the years passed, I became more and more frustrated with astrology and the astrological interpretation of Gann's work. Through my continued study and application the astrological techniques were not showing consistent results for me. I began to feel like something was missing and was questioning whether I was wasting my time. Fortunately, before giving it all up, I came across a little known article that Gann wrote for the *Milwaukee Sentinel* Magazine dated January 5, 1919. In this article, Gann says,

> "In making my predictions I use geometry and mathematics just as an astronomer does, based on immutable laws which I have discovered. . . Some weeks ago I read an interesting article on the failure of astrologers in their predictions regarding the war. Now there is a great deal in the vibrations of the planets, but to make accurate predictions the great law behind it all, which the ancients understood, but which they purposely refrained from putting in their books, as they wanted to keep the secret for themselves, must enter into the calculation. That is why astrology fails, for nothing can be accurate that is not based on mathematics – and so few astrologers are mathematicians."

So here we have Gann telling us quite explicitly that in order to make accurate predictions something else must enter the calculation and that this is why astrology fails. Yet, most if not all of the Gann material out there is based on some type of astrological interpretation.

Even in Gann's novel, *The Tunnel Thru the Air*, the opening paragraph of the seventh chapter on future cycles is a carbon copy of the first sentence from the quote above. In the novel, the main character Robert Gordon says, "My calculations are based on the cycle theory and on mathematical sequences." If he was using astrology, I would think it would

INTRODUCTION

read a little different. Perhaps, "My calculations are based on astrology." Although the main character in the novel is said to be a great believer in astrology and knew that the Bible was replete with references that the heavens ruled, he takes it upon himself to go see Professor O. B. Joyful in the hope that the great science of astrology would throw some light upon the disappearance of Marie, the love of his life. Think about this, if Robert Gordon was using the same astrological techniques as the Astrologer, Professor O.B. Joyful, to forecast the movements of stocks and commodities, wouldn't you think that he could do that himself. Taking into consideration all of the above, we have to come to the conclusion that he wasn't solely using astrology. If we are truly to understand the foundation of what Gann was doing, we have to come to grips with this, and it is my opinion that this 1919 article is the key.

In the 1919 article, Gann makes some predictions about the German Kaiser Wilhelm Hohenzollern, and provides some details as to how he made his predictions. We have to come to the realization that there is no difference in the method that Gann used to forecast events for individuals and those that he used for stocks. If we can use this article to ascertain how he made forecasts for the German Kaiser, then maybe this will provide clues as to how he did it for stocks and commodities. Thus, my main goal for this book is to take an in depth look at the forecasts and statements that Gann makes in this article, and to offer explanations as to how he was able to come to these conclusions. This article will force us to look at subjects such as arithmancy or numerology, periodicity, cycles, and geometry to analyze its contents. Although this work is brief and to the point, it is my hope that this will throw light on the numerous theories written about Gann techniques and methods, and induce further research into the concepts presented herein.

Awodele,
Union, KY

June 6, 2013

PERSONAL NOTE

The Author of *W.D. Gann: Divination by Mathematics* will be pleased to receive any communication concerning the contents of this book.

E-mail: BEKHLLC@outlook.com

1

W.D. Gann

For the majority of people who read this book, I expect that they will most likely already know a lot about W.D. Gann, but for those who do not, it is necessary to give a little background information about his accomplishments and work. William Delbert Gann was born on June 6, 1878 in Lufkin, Texas. In his promotional booklet issued in 1954, it says that he made his first trade in commodities on August 15, 1902, but his fame spread as a result of the December 1909 *Ticker and Investment Digest* magazine article written by R.D. Wyckoff, who was owner of the magazine at that time. In this article, he talks about what he calls The Law of Vibration and how it enables him to accurately predict the points at which stocks will rise and fall. Numerous examples are given in the article where Gann predicts that a stock would not go higher or lower than a certain price. It goes on to say that in the presence of a representative of the *Ticker and Investment Digest* magazine during the month of October 1909, Gann made 286 transactions in various stocks during 25 market days and that 240 of the 286 transactions were profitable. It says that the capital with which he operated was doubled ten times so that at the end of the month he had 1,000 percent of his original margin.

In 1909, prior to this magazine article, there was a series of advertisements posted in the New York Herald that make claims similar to those of W.D. Gann. The advertisements only provide a business name with the title "OROLO" along with a street address. Although there is no authorship attached, we know that they were made by Gann based on their content. In one advertisement dated Sunday April 18, 1909, the author states,

> "I have proved after nine years of scientific investigation that it is possible to know every move the markets make. It is a scientific problem, not guess work, as many believe. I have investigated all "Systems," found most of them worthless to the average trader and none of them perfect. I investigated astrology and kindred sciences to learn the law of the movements in the markets. In them all there was something lacking, and not until I struck upon the law of vibration and attraction as applied in Wireless Telegraphy did I find the key to Wall Street. I find the different stocks grouped into families, each having its own distinct vibration, which acts sympathetically upon others of the group and causes them to move in unison. I now have perfected my theory until I can forecast every move in Stocks, Cotton and Wheat."

We see in this passage that he also makes a reference to astrology, and says specifically that after its investigation into the movements of the market, he found that something was lacking. Then, he hints upon the fact that it was not until he struck upon the Law of Vibration that he found the key to Wall Street. If we want to truly understand what the Law of Vibration really is, we have to move away from astrology.

Back to the subject at hand, we see that Gann comes on the scene with these advertisements prior to the *Ticker and Investment Digest* magazine article dated December, 1909. In fact, he perfected his method as early as 1908. In his promotional booklet entitled, *Why Money is Lost on Commodities and Stocks and How to Make Profits* from 1954, it records the following:

> "1908 May 12th left Oklahoma City for New York City. August 8th made one of his greatest mathematical discoveries for predicting the trend of stocks and commodities. Started trading with a capital of $300 and made $25,000. Started another account with $130 and made $12,000 in thirty days time."

Now that we know a little about W.D. Gann and his background, the next piece of pertinent information is the contents of the 1919 article from the *Milwaukee Sentinel* magazine. This you will find in the second chapter. It will provide you with a foundation for the material to be discussed in subsequent chapters as I will make references to various sections from this article as we proceed throughout the remainder of this book.

2

The 1919 Article

Sees the Kaiser Shot While Trying to Flee His Prison

Student of the Law of Vibration, Who Also Is a Prophet of Note and a Seer of First Quality, Makes Another Prediction Regarding the Fate of the Man Named Hohenzollern, Who Until Late Said He Was the Great War Lord and Also the Most High Admiral of the Atlantic.

There is nothing to anything save and except the Law of Vibration. Vibration is fundamental, exact, universal. Nothing is exempt from it. You can watch it carefully and then own all the money in the world. You can study it for a few decades and become a prophet. You can predict events – before or after – you can become a first or second guesser just as you choose. You can even foretell what is going to be done with the man named Hohenzollern, who once was a Great War Lord and Most High Admiral of the Atlantic.

And it is all SO simple.

This is the secret of the Law of Vibration:-

Find exactly by a study of geometrical angles what is meant by each letter in a man's name and his destiny is at once an open book to you. The same goes in regard to countries and rulers. That is all there is to it.

Now, to explain:-

William D. Gann, a Wall street broker, is the discoverer of the Law of Vibration and its application to matters mundane. In its particular relation to the man Hohenzollern Mr. Gann wrote as follows for this Magazine:-

"Wilhelm Hohenzollern, the infamous imperial scoundrel, whose crimes against women and children have debauched and shocked the civilized world and caused him to be the most hated and despised man in history, was born January 27, 1859. His mother, Princess Victoria Adelaide Mary Louisa Wettin, was born November 21, 1840.

"A study of the mother's maiden name, which always reveals the secret nature and future destiny of the male child more than the father's name, indicates the remarkable events in the Kaiser's life. Her name shows that the husband lacked love and sympathy for her, which is fully manifested in the depraved feelings and unsympathetic nature of her son. The name Hohenzollern shows that he would inherit from his father an unbalanced mind; that he would be an egotist, a braggart and a selfish coward. No one doubts that none other than a depraved and insane mind could have conceived the idea of world dominion. No sane man would have antagonized the United States and believed he could defeat the country whose colors have never yet trailed the dust.

"His name and numbers indicated that he would inherit a throne, property and wealth and then lose them all in his own acts. His numbers reveal the fact that all vain hopes would be defeated in the end.

"The letter W is a twin letter or a letter with a dual nature. While it is one of justice and fairness, when afflicted it becomes one of the most selfish and debased influences. The letter N is the most powerful letter for producing wealth and fame, especially when the surname begins with W and ends with N. It overcomes all obstacles and wins in the end. A name ending with N leaves a record which is famous long after death, as in the case of George Washington, Abraham Lincoln, Duke of Wellington and Woodrow Wilson. When H is the initial letter, it attempts to create a position of wealth and power through destruction. It afflicts or opposes W and N. The evil tendencies Wilhelm Hohenzollern inherited from his father's name caused him to break the heart of his mother, whose noble qualities were shown by the fact that her name began with W and ended with N. Had the former Kaiser understood the science of letters and numbers he would have realized that he would meet his Waterloo through Woodrow Wilson, whose names stands for justice and liberty.

"The numbers '5', '7' and '9' are very unfavorable for him. The fifth, seventh and ninth months of the year, as well as the fifth, seventh and ninth months from his birthday, are very evil and eventful in his life. Observe that he abdicated on his evil day, the ninth, in his evil month, November.

"His sixty-first year, 1919, will prove to be the most unfortunate in his career, and I very seriously doubt if he will live to see the end of the year. He will suffer the almost complete loss of his wealth. The death of one of his sons, probably the Crown Prince, is indicated. There is also danger of imprisonment and severe illness. The following are his most evil periods for this year:- March 20 to 27, May 10 to 14, July 2 to 5, August 23 to 25, October 10 to 13 and November 7 to 13.

"From January 27, his birthday, until February 9, will prove to be a very unfortunate period, when he will be sick in mind and body. He will have thoughts of taking his life and may attempt it. The Allies will probably ask for his extradition.

"Three critical periods are indicated:-

"April 9 to May 9 will be one of the most unfavorable periods, when his life and liberty will be seriously threatened. His health will be very bad and his mind almost unbalanced. He will probably be brought to trial at this time, and if he receives the sentence it will possibly prove to be his death blow.

"August will be most unfortunate. He will be much depressed from imprisonment or restraint. He will meet with opposition on every hand and reap as he has sown.

"October and November are the most evil months. This third period will be most fatal and there is strong evidence that if he is still alive a violent death may take place.

"His name reveals strong testimony that when brought to trial the death penalty will be inflicted, unless Woodrow Wilson intercedes in his behalf and on humane principles asks for life imprisonment, and it is strongly indicated that he will. It is a sure thing that the Kaiser will receive extreme punishment and spend the balance of his life under limitations and restraints. He will be confined either in a prison or an asylum. The end will come suddenly and not be a natural death. There is an indication that he will make an attempt to escape but in so doing will lose his life."

Mr. Gann is unknown to the general public, but his name and personality have long been familiar to Wall street. He predicted both elections of President Wilson when the judgment of keen, shrewd men favored that of his opponent. He foretold the end of the world war and the abdication of the Kaiser to the day it occurred, and his predictions regarding the movements of big stocks have been for years the talk of the brokers.

Mr. Gann is modest and unassuming and looks more like a deep student than the financier, as the public mind usually portrays him. When asked about his discovery and his predictions he tried to evade the subject at first but finally agreed to tell something about his work. He made his discovery about twenty years ago, after weeks and months of research into geometry and mathematics in ancient books and at a cost of $25,000.

W.D. GANN: DIVINATION BY MATHEMATICS

He consumed eighty pounds of paper in figuring, and his geometrical deductions and calculations are contained on a roll which, when unwound, would reach from Wall street to the Battery. From all these numbers Mr. Gann erects his geometrical figures. He has a big, ponderous volume filled with these figures – squares, angles, pyramids and circles – and whenever he wants to know anything he turns to a certain geometrical figure and puts his finger on the answer.

Mr. Gann, who is a native of Texas, gave the following account of his experience and methods:-

"It is impossible now to give any adequate idea of the law of vibration as I apply it to my business: however, the layman may be able to grasp some of the principles when I state that this is the fundamental law upon which wireless telegraphy, wireless telephones, phonographs and all other great inventions are based. Without the existence of this law these inventions would have been impossible.

"In order to test my idea I have no only put in years of labor in the regular way but I spent nine months working night and day in the old Astor Library and in the British Museum, in London, poring over ancient books on mathematics and geometry as well as the records of stock transactions as far back as 1820. I have, incidentally, examined the manipulations of Jay Gould, Daniel Drew, Commodore Vanderbilt and all other important Wall street manipulators from that time to the present time.

"Vibration is fundamental; nothing is exempt from this law; it is universal, therefore applicable to every class of phenomena, animate or inanimate, on the globe."

Mr. Gann added that his researches showed that the ancients had knowledge of natural laws of which we can scarcely dream; that in a sense they were wiser than we are to-day. The fact that the ancients wrote their numbers and letters in geometrical figures opened the way to his discovery of the law that rules all things. He found that every letter and every number was written in a geometrical angle that determined the power of its vibration. Knowing the vibration in the letters of an individual's name, in the letters contained in the name of a stock or in the letters of the name of a country or a ruler, the destiny of that individual, that stock or that ruler and country can be correctly seen.

"There is everything in a name or in a word," said Mr. Gann, the strong lines of his face relaxing in a genial smile, "despite all that Shakespeare has said. There is no such thing as chance in this universe, and the names which we give to our children are governed by this great law. We have all heard the story of Voltaire, who only became great and famous after he had changed his name to what we know it to-day. Perhaps he was adept in the workings of this law."

THE 1919 ARTICLE

Mr. Gann was asked how he made his remarkable predictions regarding the Kaiser and how he determined the exact days mentioned.

"By the letters of his name and the name of his mother," he replied. "In this manner the fate of any individual can be told. The first thing I do is to get the mathematical angle, the length of the angle of his or her name and then that of the mother's name. Then you get the angle of the father's name, because that name you carry through life. Following this I take the Christian or given name, which is forced on you, so to speak, and calculate whether it is harmonious or inharmonious. There are just two things to everything – harmony or inharmony, positive or negative, light or darkness, beauty or ugliness. If the name given you is out of harmony then you have got to work through that until you have come into harmony. The given name gives the vibration set up in the body. Everything is based absolutely on geometry and mathematics. You have got to prove everything in a circle, in a square or in an angle. You have got to know how a pyramid stands to a circle, a circle to a square and how they all 'match up.'"

Speaking of the vibratory power of letters, Mr. Gann made out a list of the names of the Presidents of the United States. The letters W and N, he said is of a dual nature, and the ancients so indicated it in their original symbol. It is the most powerful letter according to its position in a name. It works either for justice and the loftiest ideals, or it tends to destruction and ruin. A person whose name begins with a W and terminates in an N will hold a most exalted position in life and wield great power. As an example, such a name and career was that of Washington who established the Union, and going down the whole list of Presidents that combination of letters does not occur again until we reach the name of Woodrow Wilson. The glance over the following names of Presidents will show this:-

George Washingon,
John Adams,
Thomas Jefferson,
James Madison,
James Monroe,
John Q. Adams,
Andrew Jackson,
M. Van Buren,
Wm. H. Harrison,
John Tyler,
James K. Polk,

James Buchanan,
Abraham Lincoln,
Andrew Johnson,
U. S. Grant,
R. B. Hayes,
James A. Garfield,
Chester A. Arthur,
Grover Cleveland,
Benjamin Harrison,
Grover Cleveland,
William McKinley,

W.D. GANN: DIVINATION BY MATHEMATICS

Z. Taylor,
Millard Filmore,
Franklin Pierce,

Theodore Roosevelt,
William H. Taft,
Woodrow Wilson.

President Wilson's name, Mr. Gann says, is even more potent than that of Washington, for his given name also begins with a "W," and his position in the world to-day is the materialization of the great vibratory power that is inherent in these letters.

In the list of Presidents it will be noted that where the "W" does not appear the letter "N" plays an important role; such as for instance, the names of Jefferson, Madison, Andrew Jackson, Lincoln – which contained two "N's" – and so on.

As another striking example of the power of these letters, Mr. Gann cited that of Napoleon, whose name began with an "N" and ended with it. Here was a combination hard to beat, but he was beaten, and by none other than Wellington, the "W" and "N" combination – the beginning and the end. It must be remembered, however, that not all persons whose names may be Wilson, or Lincoln or Wellington will be equally as great. They will more or less play an important part in their various spheres, but the date of birth is what determines the other angle and also complete the circle or the square. From all this data Mr. Gann calculates the "key number" which governs him through life. That "key number" is the whole secret of Mr. Gann's discovery, and this secret he keeps within himself. For instance, the "key number of President Wilson's name is "28," and curiously enough he is the twenty-eighth President of these United States. Therefore, the numbers "2" and "8," or their total "10," will show events of importance in Mr. Wilson's career.

Another instance of a man of prominence in this country who has wielded a powerful influence is that of Henry Watterson, editor emeritus of the Louisville Courier-Journal, whose name begins with a W and terminates in an N. And so it will be seen that in all names of prominent persons in every walk of life the W and N are rarely absent, and in cases of big men where neither letter appears in the Christian or given name the key will be found in the day and year of birth.

Mr. Gann does not care much for money except to meet his daily needs, and these are simple. He made a fortune simply that he might have the leisure necessary for him to follow his ambition – to study mathematics and delve into the knowledge held by the ancients. He does not want to be regarded as a prophet or a seer, but rather as a man of science.

"An astronomer can predict to the minute when an eclipse is going to occur," he said, "but you would not consider him a prophet, would you? Of course not. He simply makes use of mathematics based on known laws of the movements of the planets in their orbits. I have found in my researches that the Chinese understood all those laws and computed the coming of eclipses thousands of years before the Egyptians and Chaldeans. It is marvelous the knowledge that these ancients had. In making my predictions I use geometry and mathematics just as an astronomer does, based on immutable laws which I have discovered. There is nothing supernatural or weird about it. Some weeks ago I read an interesting article on the failure of astrologers in their predictions regarding the war.

Now there is a great deal in the vibrations of the planets, but to make accurate predictions the great law behind it all, which the ancients understood, but which they purposely refrained from putting in their books, as they wanted to keep the secret for themselves, must enter into the calculation. That is why astrology fails, for nothing can be accurate that is not based on mathematics – and so few astrologers are mathematicians.

"In March last several of my friends in Wall street asked me why I did not make a prediction on how long the war would last. I had been quite busy all along with my regular work in Wall street, and my evenings were given to calculating events for friends."

Mr. Gann here lifted a large bundle of letters from his desk. They were from men of prominence all over the country – from Governors of States, big public men in Washington and others, thanking him for his kindness in working out a geometrical figure of their lives and commenting upon his amazing accuracy.

"These are the things that keep me busy," he added, with a laugh. "But it is what I like to do; it is my play, my recreation. However, I went to work on that end-of-the-war calculation, and on April 4 I sent out a typewritten statement to my friends. Well, the result is known now.

"The United States went into the war on April 6. April has always been very eventful in the history of this country. Fort Sumter was fired on in the month of April, and if you will look back over history you will find that many of the important events begin or end during the month of April. I soon found that the letters and numbers in the names of President Wilson and the Kaiser revealed some very remarkable indications. Strangely enough I found that the numbers '5,' '7' and '9' are very eventful and important in the history of this country. These same numbers are fatal numbers for Kaiser Wilhelm, and showed that his evil months this year were October and November. With all the 'N's' in his name he could not beat that powerful 'W' and 'N' combination, nor could Napoleon.

"We cannot work against the law, but we can work with the law. For instance, one of my friends came to me recently very much depressed. I found he was passing through a hard period. Health and business were affected. I again tested my discovery. I told him

3

The Science of Letters & Numbers

Numerology, or the study of numbers, is one of the subjects that Gann had on his recommended reading lists. Now there are a number of lists that have been published on the internet, but unfortunately, it has been suggested that some dishonest individuals have added books that were not on any of Gann's recommended reading lists, and sell those books at inflated prices to take advantage of those who are researching Gann's methods. I have found on the following website, http://www.bonniehill.net/pages/w.d.gann.html#list, a copy of the actual Gann Reading List, which shows his Florida address in the letterhead, and another is based on the Gann Reading List from a Gann collection purchased from Ed Lambert of Lambert-Gann publishing in 1976. According to these lists, the books that Gann recommended for numerology studies are as follows:

Numerology by Clifford W. Cheasley
Philosophy of Numbers by Mrs. L. Dow Balliett
Number Vibration in Questions and Answers by Mrs. L. Dow Balliett
The Day of Wisdom According to Number Vibration by Mrs. L. Dow Balliett
The Kabala of Numbers by Sepharial (How and Why Numbers Work)
How to Play the Races and Win by Mark Mellen
The Kabala of Numbers by Sepharial (Interpretation)

W.D. GANN: DIVINATION BY MATHEMATICS

The Mysteries of Sound and Number by Sheikh Habeeb Ahmed
Numerology for Everybody – [No author is listed]
The Tarot of the Bohemians by Papus
The Power of Numbers by Numero
Numerology Made Plain by Ariel Yvon Taylor

I have managed to obtain copies of all but two of the books on the list above, and have studied them all in detail. I have even obtained books by these same authors that are not on the list, and I can honestly say that not in any one of these books are there any clues as to the reasons behind Gann's statements in the *Milwaukee Sentinel* article from 1919. Furthermore, if you have studied the books on the list just like me, you will no doubt find that just in this list of books alone, we have several different systems of numerology & techniques being expounded on. Therefore, if one were to go by this list, they would be greatly confused as to which system of number to letter relationships and techniques to utilize in order to duplicate what Gann was doing.

Was it based on the phonetics or the sound of the name as detailed in *The Mysteries of Sound and Number* by Sheikh Habeeb Ahmed? Do you just add the numbers up in a name to get a numerical value or do you pyramid as described by Numero? Do you add the consonants and vowels separately? Believe me, I've tried it all. I have even expanded my research to include numerology books by authors who are not on the recommended reading list, but it was not until I was reviewing the promotional booklet issued by Gann in 1954 did I find a most valuable clue.

As I referenced in the first chapter, the booklet is entitled, *Why Money is Lost on Commodities and Stocks and How to Make Profits*, and it details some of Gann's major accomplishments along with some details of his trading record. What really grabbed my attention is one particular statement towards the end of the booklet in what appears to be an advertisement for his Master Calculator. Under item number 8, it says,

> "The Master Calculator locates the Corner Stone, the Key Stone and the Cap Stone for Price and Time Trend."

It caught my attention because I remembered seeing these terms in a book on the subject matter at hand that was not on the Gann recommended reading list. I did a quick search on the internet and found that each of these "Stones" are referenced in the Bible, and I have found many books that specifically refer to their usage with respect to Solomon's temple. In addition, I have found material where these terms are used in Masonry,

THE SCIENCE OF LETTERS & NUMBERS

of which we know that Gann was affiliated with, but the main thing is that I remembered seeing these terms in a book entitled, *The Ancient Science of Numbers* by Luo Clement.

In the 1954 booklet, Gann uses these terms to describe locations of price and time trend, and in Clement's book we find that they are used to describe the position or location of letters in a name. Furthermore, I remembered that this same book was referenced in a 1909 article about the science of letters and numbers. This is all thanks to the publication of a free e-book called, *The Aso-Neith Cryptogram* by Romeman. In this e-book there are a series of articles & advertisements about the system of numbers that were utilized by an Asenath Williams Woodcock Cochran. A number of these articles, and more, can be found by searching online. Needless to say, I went back to studying Clement's book and the Aso-Neith articles with a new found interest, and what I hadn't seen before, I was now able to see. There is no doubt in my mind that the foundation of the system of numbers and letters that Gann utilizes in the 1919 article came from the teachings of the Aso-Neith Cryptogram.

This Aso-Neith Cryptogram e-book shows that as early as March 29, 1903, which is the date of the oldest article in the e-book, the so-called Pythagorean number to letter assignments were being utilized by Aso-Neith in her work. I find it interesting that in the many books on numerology that I have in my possession, when referring to the pioneer of the Pythagorean system, Mrs. L. Dow Balliett's name is the one that comes up. I have read material that says she first applied the principles of Pythagoras to the English language around 1903, but I have yet to find any validation for this claim. The first book that she published on numerology that I can find was in 1905 entitled, *"How to Attain Success Through the Strength of Vibration: A System of Numbers as Taught by Pythagoras"*. So why is there no mention of Aso-Neith in the history of Numerology as it applies to Pythagorean number to letter assignments?

Reading the series of articles in the e-book, you can't help but notice that they sound curiously similar to the writings of Gann. For example, in an article dated March 14, 1909 in *The Plain Dealer* of Cleveland, OH on page 52, Mrs. Aso-Neith says,

> "it is an old, old science. It was known to the ancients. Mention of it is made in the Bible. . . When asked to explain this Cryptogram Mrs. Cochran refuses, saying it is her secret. But there are other exponents of it who are not so secretive, and anyone who cares to take the trouble can find out all about it in a little book written by Luo Clement and published by Roger Brothers."

This book, published in 1908, predates that famous Gann interview in the *Ticker and Investment Digest* in December of 1909. This means that he would have possibly had the opportunity to be exposed to it prior to his great discovery of August 8, 1908 or even to the teachings of Aso-Neith as early as 1903.

With Clement's book, and the numerous articles that can be found on Aso-Neith, you can obtain a great understanding of the system and decipher how they applied it in many of the readings. Furthermore, you will find that it's unlike any other system of numerology in print. However, before getting into the details of the system, there is amazing evidence for its connection to Gann through some of the statements he made and their similarity to statements made by Aso-Neith at an earlier date.

Consider the following statements Gann made in the 1919 article.

> "This is the secret of the law of vibration: Find exactly by a study of geometrical angles what is meant by each letter in a man's name and his destiny is at once an open book to you. The same goes in regard to countries and rulers. That is all there is to it."

Now consider the following statements made by Aso-Neith in an article published in the *Willmar Tribune*, Wednesday, July 30, 1913.

> "When a name is given, the geometrical angles, both fluent and straight, which represent the letters, are registered on the subjective plane. They become the highways and byways upon which the individual travels through life."

Now consider the next set of statements. In the 1919 Gann article, it states,

> "He consumed eighty pounds of paper in figuring, and his geometrical deductions and calculations are contained on a roll which, when unwound, would reach from Wall Street to the Battery. From all these numbers Mr. Gann erects his geometrical figures. He has a big, ponderous volume filled with these figures – squares, angles, pyramids and circles – and whenever he wants to know anything he turns to a certain geometrical figure and puts his finger on the answer."

THE SCIENCE OF LETTERS & NUMBERS

Now consider the statements made by Aso-Neith in *The Minneapolis Journal* on July 4, 1905. It reads,

> "There is nothing occult about me or my system of prophecy, said Mrs. Cochran. I have gone further even than the prophets of old. Numbers and vibrations hold the secret of every individual and the secret of the universe. Given a name and the date of birth, I can tell everything about a person, state or nation. . . To explain Mrs. Cochran's system more elaborately, each human being is anchored in the Infinite by a certain geometrical sign which reveals a digit number. There are eight of these numbers, 9 being a composite number, the Alpha and Omega."

Just as Gann erected certain geometrical figures, Mrs. Cochran explains that every person is anchored by a geometrical sign. We can deduce that the number to which each person vibrates has a corresponding geometrical figure, and Gann possibly used these numbered figures to divine key periods in an individual's life just like he used the Price Time Charts of pyramids, hexagons, squares, etc. in his courses. However, before getting too far ahead of ourselves, the next Chapter will focus on the basics of the Aso-Neith system. This will help us to decipher how Gann used it in the 1919 article.

4

The Aso-Neith Cryptogram

Mrs. Asenath "Aso-Neith" Cochran was a music teacher who discovered or invented this system of divination. In *The [New York] Sun* dated Sunday, January 17, 1904, in an article with the heading, *Names, Numbers and Fate: More About the System that Enables One to Be His Own Prophet*, it says,

> "The woman who discovered the system, which may be called mathematical divination, relates this story in connection with its origin. She noticed, in studying musical composition and observing her pupils, that certain numbers seemed to have a uniform meaning or vibration, and also that certain letters in names seemed to be identical with these. She became so interested and impressed that she determined to give herself up for a little time to the contemplative study of it. . . as the result of this study, [she] saw how numbers and color vibrations are related to individuals. To assure herself that the system was no illusion she set about verifying it by the names and birth dates of historical characters and by those of people who were well known to her, and the results were a surprising confirmation."

As I mentioned in the previous chapter, Aso-Neith indicated that Luo Clement's book, *The Ancient Science of Numbers*, would reveal much of the system she used in her work. It is here that I would like to provide the reader with the basics of this system. First and foremost, the letters of the alphabet are arranged in degrees as shown in the following table.

1st Degree		2nd Degree		3rd Degree		Parts of Body
A	1	J	10	S	100	Head
B	2	K	20	T	200	Kidneys
C	3	L	30	U	300	Liver
D	4	M	40	V	400	Intestines
E	5	N	50	W	500	Stomach/Spine
F	6	O	60	X	600	Mental Organism
G	7	P	70	Y	700	Heart
H	8	Q	80	Z	800	Generative Organs
I	9	R	90			Nervous Organism

The letters A – I are representative of the numbers 1 – 9, the letters J – R are representative of the numbers 10 – 90 (counting by tens), and the letters S – Z are representative of the numbers 100 – 800 (counting by hundreds). Thus, each column represents a different strength or degree of vibration. Clement tells us that the "0" cipher, which indicates the strength of vibratory force, must be considered in reading the effect of the letters upon the name, however, they are not counted in the enumeration of the number of the name. Then, he gives an example indicating that "J" will exert a greater force in the shaping of events and character than "A", and "S" will be still more forceful than "J", but when calculating the name they all have the value of "1".

THE NAME NUMBER

The first component to calculate in this system is the Name Number, which is described as a positive force. In order to calculate it, he instructs us to write down the numerical value of each letter composing the name, and add these numbers together. If the result is greater than 9, we reduce further by adding the two digits together until we obtain a single digit. As an example, he enumerates the name Anna in his book.

W.D. GANN: DIVINATION BY MATHEMATICS

```
A   N   N   A
1   5   5   1   =   12
```

Since 12 is greater than 9, it is further reduced by adding its two digits where 1 + 2 = 3. As the great positive force, the Name Number asserts itself in the general affairs of life – social, domestic, and business. It is the most powerful spiritual energy in the shaping of material things. He also says that the given name exerts the most powerful influence in shaping the life of every individual, but the character of the influence depends largely on the degree of harmony which may exist between it and the Birth Number, which is simply the day of the individual's birth. This is the second component to consider in the system.

THE BIRTH NUMBER

According to Clement's book, the Birth Number is the great negative force and works directly on the body – affecting the health of the individual according to the position that it occupies in relation to the Name Number. If these two are inharmonious, they would tend to produce equally inharmonious conditions in the particular portion of the body governed by the Birth number, and sickness, when it came, would naturally go to these points of least resistance.

To ascertain to what degree the two numbers are harmonious or inharmonious, the nine lines of letters in the Vibration Table are divided into three distinct classes, designated as Triads. Letters with a numerical value of 1, 5, or 7 compose the First Triad, letters with a numerical value of 2, 4, or 8 compose the Second Triad, and letters with a numerical value of 3, 6, or 9 compose the Third Triad.

TRIADS		LETTERS	BODY PART
1st	1, 5, 7	(A, J, S), (E, N, W), (G, P, Y)	Governs upper part of body
2nd	2, 4, 8	(B, K, T), (D, M, V), (H, Q, Z)	Controls lower part of body
3rd	3, 6, 9	(C, L, U), (F, O, X), (I, R)	Liver, mental, nervous sys.

This means that A, J, and S, each of whose numerical value is 1, is in harmony with the letters E, N, and W, each of whose numerical value is 5, and also, G, P, and Y, each of whose numerical value is 7. Letters that are not in the same Triad are said to bear an inharmonious relationship with each other, but there are additional factors to consider in ascertaining how inharmonious they are. This will be discussed later in the chapter.

THE ASO-NEITH CRYPTOGRAM

One of the most important teachings of the Aso-Neith system is that the Name Number should be in harmony with the Birth Number. Thus, when it is in harmony it is said to be in concord with the Birth Number. In the various articles about the Aso-Neith system, you will find many references where she assigns an individual a new name that is in concord with their Birth Number. This is due to the fact that when the concord does not exist between the two, the influence of the name on the thoughts and acts of the individual is always discordant. As a natural result, failure follows instead of success, sickness comes in the place of health, and troubles and sorrows rather than peace and happiness. Thus, at a very basic level, one of the major goals was to change the name so that its numerical value would be in harmony with the Birth Number.

For example, given the name Aso-Neith who Mrs. Cochran went by, I would expect its numerical value to be in harmony with her day of birth, which was June 16, 1851. The numerical value of the day, being a two digit number, would be further reduced by adding 1 + 6 to get 7. This is her Birth Number. Now we will enumerate the Name, which we expect to be in the 1, 5, 7 concord.

```
A  S  O  N  E  I  T  H
1  1  6  5  5  9  2  8  =  37  =  10  =  1
```

It is indeed in the 1,5,7 concord. We also know from the articles that Aso-Neith took on another name, which was Neypa. Let's see if this name is also part of the concord.

```
N  E  Y  P  A
5  5  7  7  1  =  25  =  7
```

So we can see that the "7" is also in harmony with the 1, 5, 7 concord. Furthermore, notice that every letter within the name NEYPA "55771" is also part of the concord, which also comes into play with additional aspects of the system. As for the address where she conducted her business, we find in one article that it was located at 514 West One Hundred and Fourteenth Street, Manhattan. If you add these numbers, 5 + 1 + 4 + 1 + 1 + 4 = 16 = 7, we find that it is also in the concord. As expected, she was making use of the system in her own life. Now, what if I told you that it is possible to see this same use in Gann's life and work? Would you be surprised? Let's take a look.

Now, if what I am suggesting in this book, that Gann was using this system in the 1919 article, then it would not be farfetched to see the use of this system in his own life. Consider the fact that if someone was convinced through application of the system on historical figures, friends, etc. that the system worked, then wouldn't you think they would change their name to harmonize with their day of birth? Now we know Gann was born June 6, 1878, so according to the Aso-Neith system his birth number is 6, and it belongs to the 3, 6, 9 Triad. We know that Gann was born with the name William, which enumerates to 34 as shown below.

```
W   I   L   L   I   A   M
5   9   3   3   9   1   4   =   34   =   7
```

Through further reduction it reduces to a "7" (3 + 4), and we see that it is not in harmony with his concord. However, Gann always used the name W.D. Gann. Enumerating the name W.D. Gann gives a numerical value of 27.

```
W   D       G   A   N   N
5   4       7   1   5   5   =   27   =   9
```

Through further reduction, 2 + 7 = 9, and it is now in harmony with the concord. Even if we enumerate each name separately, the initials "W.D." add up to 9, and "Gann" adds up to 18, which also further reduces to 9. Coincidence? Maybe, maybe not. Let's look further.

In another e-book published by Romeman entitled, *Who Was OROLO?*, there are a series of New York Herald advertisements from April to December 1908 where an unnamed individual makes statements in these articles similar to those of W.D. Gann in his later writings. Even though no name is attached to the advertisements, there is overwhelming evidence that Gann published them. In these advertisements, it was the name of the business that was listed as OROLO. If we take this name and calculate its numerical value, we find that it is in harmony with Gann's Birth Number.

```
O   R   O   L   O
6   9   6   3   9   =   33   =   6
```

The numerical value of the name OROLO is 33, which reduces to a 6. So we have to ask, did Gann, who was more than likely conversant with the Aso-Neith system, decide to make this the name of his business because he knew that it would harmonize with his Birth Number? Furthermore, just like we saw in the name Neypa on the previous page, all of the letters in this name are in the 3, 6, 9 concord.

Now, as already shown in the example with Aso-Neith, in another aspect of the system as expounded in one of her articles, we find that the street and office number for the place of business should also harmonize with the Birth Number in order to bring success. In *The [New York] Sun*, Sunday, January 17, 1904 it reads,

"When she [Aso-Neith] had studied his name and birth dates, she asked him where he was doing business. He told her at 71 Broadway, and gave the number of his office. You might as well, said she, expect to send a message across the Atlantic by tapping the Morse alphabet on a table as to hope to make a success of anything you undertake there. Your leading number is 7, the others are 10, 5, and 3. Now, you are under 8, which has no relation to any of them, for none of them is even a factor of it. Broadway is 8 and the street number and your office number, when added to get the digit, each make 9. This gives you constant, unrelieved opposition, which you cannot overcome. . . She told him to get an office at 52, or some other number which added would make 7, or at least, one of his numbers, or some number in harmony with them."

Now what would you say if OROLO's office number as listed in the advertisements is also in harmony with Gann's concord of 3, 6, 9? At the end of every advertisement, the address listed was OROLO, 120 Liberty st. Thus, 1 + 2 + 0 = 3, and it is in harmony with the concord. Furthermore, in a couple of these advertisements, the address was listed as OROLO, 120 Liberty st., room 1,206. If you add up the digits to the room number you get 9, and any number added to 9 will still reduce to itself. Thus, 3 + 9 = 12, and 1 + 2 = 3. The Street and room number is still in harmony with the 3, 6, 9 concord.

If we take a further look at the various offices where Gann conducted his business throughout the course of his career, we find in many instances these values are also in harmony with his concord. On various Gann letterheads we find a number of different addresses. One address is listed as 82 Wall Street New York 5. N.Y. If you add the numbers in this address, 8 + 2 + 5 you get 15, which reduces to 6 (1 + 5). Another address he had was 820 S.W. 26th Road Miami, Florida. When you add these values, 8 + 2 + 2 + 6 you get 18, which reduces to 9 (1 + 8). In another letterhead dated May 4, 1949 the Miami address is listed as 820 S.W. 26th road Miami 45. Florida. This is the same address as before, but the 45 is added to this one. We know that 9 added to any number will still equal the number when reduced to its root digit, so it will still be 9. On another letterhead we have an address of 78 Wall Street New York. The number 7 + 8 is 15, which reduces to 6. It is my belief that Gann purposefully attempted to select the street and office numbers where he conducted his business so that they would be in harmony with his concord per the Aso-Neith system. Of course we can find addresses where they don't harmonize with his concord, but I don't find that this invalidates the theory put forth thus far. In many instances I would think it would be very difficult to find a location that exactly harmonizes with your concord in all instances. Furthermore, we have much more evidence to present as we proceed throughout the remainder of this book.

Since we can find evidence of the basics of the Aso-Neith system in the life of Gann, we should also expect to find it in his writings. Specifically, I would expect to find it in his novel, *The Tunnel Thru the Air or Looking Back From 1940* with respect to its main character, Robert Gordon. On the first page we are given the date of Robert's birth, which is June 9, 1906. Right off, we have a Birth Number of 9, which just so happens to be in the same 3, 6, 9 concord of Gann's own birth Number. Next, let's find the numerical value of Robert's name.

```
R  O  B  E  R  T
9  6  2  5  9  2  =  33  =  6
```

It is 33, which happens to be the same numerical value of the business name OROLO, which further reduces to a 6. So for Robert, the main character in the novel, he has a Birth Number of 9, and a Name Number of 6. To put the icing on the cake so to speak, there is a passage in the novel on page 194 that reads,

> "A few days after New York's reception to Colonel Lindbergh, Robert decided to get down to business. He visited his brokers in Wall Street, talked over the market situation and found that they did not agree with his ideas and views. Decided to open an office at 69 Wall Street, and Walter was to work with him when he had time from his studies."

These are the very numbers that make up the Birth & Name Number, and when they are added together, 6 + 9 = 15, and 1 + 5 = 6. Once again, everything harmonizes with the concord.

Now it says that Walter was to work with Robert when he had time from his studies, and it goes on to say,

> "They consulted about a stenographer or office assistant. Walter had met Miss Edna Quinton, a very talented girl, whom he thought was the most competent he had ever known, so Robert gave her a position in his office."

The numerical value of Edna's given name is as follows:

```
E  D  N  A
5  4  5  1  =  15  =  6
```

Through further reduction, 1 + 5 = 6. So we have an individual who is working closely in the office with Robert whose name is in harmony with his concord. This is no doubt designed to create a harmonious working environment.

In *The [New York] Sun*, on Sunday, March 29, 1903, in regards to an article on the Aso-Neith system of divination by numbers, the narrator of the article is recounting an instance when a friend by the name of "Richards" is sad, and Richards informs him that things were not going well for him ever since he moved into his new offices. Another friend suggested that perhaps he was under the wrong numbers. The article goes on to say that

> "Richards went to the woman [Aso-Neith] who got up the system, and she told him he would never be successful at the number where he was located and he must move. He had a long lease, and there were other reasons why it was impossible for him to do so. He asked her if there was not some way out of it, and she suggested that if he had a partner whose numbers were in accord with the number of his offices to take charge of a part of the business which she indicated, the difficulty would be, in part at least, overcome. He and Carter had been talking of a partnership. The woman worked out Carter's numbers, found they were all right, the partnership was formed and business has been going all right ever since."

It's the same theme from the novel. Gann simply veiled the fact that Robert opened offices at 69 Wall Street and hired an assistant to work in the office that also harmonized with his 3,6,9 concord. All of what has been spoken of thus far is related to the Aso-Neith not to invest or speculate in any stock that was due for a rise, for he was bound to lose, but advised him to select a stock that was itself depressed and sell short. He did this and made money in a time when conditions were against him. That is what I mean by working with the law."

* * * *

Now that you have read the article above and have an idea of its contents, we will proceed with our analysis of Gann's statements and comments within this article, with the goal of showing how he was able to come to these conclusions. However, in order to do this we need to first understand what Gann meant by the statement, "*Had the former Kaiser understood the science of letters and numbers . . .*" This is connected to the numerology of the name.

system and Luo Clement's book. We can even look at Clement's name and see that the same theme is present.

```
L  U  O
3  3  6  =  12  =  3

C  L  E  M  E  N  T
3  3  5  4  5  5  2  =  27  =  9
```

His first name is obviously constructed so that each of the letter's is also in the Triad, which comes into play when you consider the cycles. However, before digressing too much, let us continue with the goal of this chapter, which is to provide the details of the Aso-Neith system.

Thus far, we have only reviewed the basics of the Aso-Neith system. We learned how the numbers were assigned to the letters, the force of vibration that each letter carries, how to calculate the Name Number, how to determine the Birth Number, and which numbers and letters form a concord with each other. To proceed further, we need to learn a little more about the Name Number and Birth Number. We learned that it was important that the Birth & Name number be in harmony for success & health, but we know that in many instances this is not the case. On page 29, Clement tells us that,

> ". . . it does not necessarily follow that, because the NAME AND BIRTH NUMBERS are inharmonious, the individual who is subject to such conditions must suffer from continued poor health. If the vibrations of the NAME NUMBER are very strong, and other conditions (to be explained later) are harmonious, sickness may be avoided for a long period. In fact, it is possible, even under these conditions, that an individual may become abnormally healthy."

The point being made is that there are other factors that play a part in how the name affects the individual in both health and personality. These are the "Cornerstone", the "Keystone", and the "Capstone".

Yes! These are the very terms that Gann uses in his 1954 promotional booklet as already mentioned in the third chapter, where he says that,

"The Master Calculator locates the Corner Stone, the Key Stone and the Cap Stone for Price and Time Trend."

In Clement's book, the Cornerstone in a name is the first or initial letter. He says that the influence of this force will be felt throughout the entire life of the individual, or object, under its vibrations. If it is in opposition to the Triad in which the Birth Number has its place, it is certain to interfere seriously with the successful culmination of every undertaking over which that discordant number can assert influence.

The Keystone in a name is the middle letter. It bears the weight of the arch, and should, therefore, be a strong Material Letter. More will be said about this later. In a name that has an even number of letters it will have no Keystone or middle letter, so it will lack its forceful vibrations.

The Capstone is the name's final letter. As the finishing or completing force, it holds the fulfillment of all the possibilities of the name. Its vibrations are among the strongest that play through the name. In selecting what he calls a perfect name, the Cornerstone, Keystone, and Capstone should also be in harmony with the Birth Number's concord. Thus, if the name has no Keystone or middle letter, it can not be a perfect name.

The Cornerstone, Keystone, and Capstone apply to the first, second, and third degrees of each number as listed in the Vibration Table respectively. The Cornerstones correspond to the letters (A-I) and to the 1st degree vibration, which are the numbers (1-9), the Keystones to the letters (J-R) corresponding to the 2nd degree, which are the numbers (10-90), and the Capstones to the letters (S-Z) corresponding to the 3rd degree, which are the numbers (100-800). This is why it says that the Capstones are among the strongest that play through the name. In addition to the above, they also apply to the numbers in each Triad as shown in the following table.

Cornerstone	Keystone	Capstone
1	5	7
2	4	8
3	6	9

Thus, 1 is the Cornerstone; 5 the Keystone, and 7 the Capstone of the 1-5-7 Triad. So also the remaining two Triads correspond in like manner.

In reading a number, we read the three degrees of vibration. That is to say, in reading a 1 or a 5, we must always lay considerable stress upon the effect of the Capstone of the Triad, the 7. So, too, we must consider the influence of the 8 in reading a 2 or a 4, and of the 9 in reading a 3 or a 6. For example, in the Triad of 3-6-9, the 9 will invariably intensify the spirituality of the 3, and will add to the steadfastness of the 6, unless its beneficent effect is sadly neutralized by a most inharmonious Birth Number.

The next piece of information that is vital to performing character analysis is the individual meanings of the letters. On page 59 Clement says,

> "The Science of Numbers teaches that each letter, or number, possesses certain distinct characteristics, and that, in accordance with the manner of the occurrence of these forces in the name and birth of the individual, such qualities manifest themselves for good or for evil."

The descriptions of the letters that follow are reproduced from Luo Clement's book, and when references were made in other parts of his text concerning a particular letter, I took the liberty to add and comment on them under the section called "Additional Notes". No doubt, as you learn more and see how each of the letters affect the lives of individuals in your own work, you can add to these descriptions, but they will more than suffice when analyzing how Gann came up with many of his conclusions in the 1919 article. There is no need to read through each description of the letters at this point, but they will serve as useful references for the remaining material in this book.

THE LAW OF THE LETTERS

A or 1. As "A" is the head letter, 1 should denote intellectuality, but intellectuality displayed in a most diverse manner. In fact, even when in harmony, an "A" usually requires several outlets for its energies, or as many as three "strings to its bow". Though a planner, and often successful in organizing and directing, its ability in this direction is that of the architect. So seldom is "A" the builder that it is pretty safe to predict that others will always have to execute the plans it outlines. The appearance of 1 in the name marks the beginning of new conditions. Even the "A" Cycle generally brings changes in life, either socially, or commercially, or both. If these changes appear under harmonious conditions they may be turned to great advantage. If left to themselves, or not directed into proper channels, they are quite as likely to result disastrously. An "A" out of harmony would be obstinate and headstrong. The tendency to "begin" things would still exist, but the power to "finish" would be weakened to correspond to the extent of vibratory discord.

Additional Notes for "A"

One who is under the Cycle of "A" will show great aversion for anything that is dark – dark colors, dark rooms, etc. The Cycle of A would bring its element of change, and the beginning of new things.

It provides the ability to plan and direct.

If A comes before a letter that is out of harmony with the birth, it will indicate important life changes, since by nature it generally brings changes in life.

Being in harmony with the birth number, it tends to nullify the material influence of the letter D if it appears in the name. It helps to bring out important changes, not only in the individual life of the bearer, but in the things in which he is most interested.

Being in harmony with the Name Number, emphasizes its characteristics, standing for intellectuality, and for originality in beginnings.

When A is prominent in a name, as the Initial Letter and perhaps recurring several times, it will be found that the person is given to taking the initiative and to working originally.

"A" as a Cornerstone: It would lead one to begin many things, but needs vibrations in the name that would help to finish them, which would be a 7, either in the Name or in the Birth Number. It is not a good Cornerstone for any person except one who is a 7 in BIRTH. However, he also says on page 124 that A would furnish the power to begin many things, while a Birth Number of 8 would impel a person to finish them. So 7 & 8. The effect of A is to bring lack of continuity. Nothing but a 7 can bring the force of completion. So if inharmonious, you can forecast that this is a person who likes to start many projects, but you don't complete them, and if they do get completed, there is someone who always lends a helping hand. If harmonious, you like to start many projects and are able to finish them as well.

B or 2. As 2 bears the message of the maternal spirit, its appearance in the name of a woman would indicate strength of mother-love. In a man it would tend to induce an interest in agriculture, horticulture, or in some other pursuit in which he might have an opportunity to assist and foster the efforts of nature. Almost invariably it invokes love of nature and domestic inclinations. Usually there is an aversion to long journeys, and, when travel is necessary, eagerness to return. In material things 2 is not strong, and its greatest achievements are frequently postponed until after the beginning of the fortieth year. Though loyal and extremely sympathetic, a 2 is apt to be strongly fixed in opinions. What these opinions may be depends largely upon the harmony of vibrations. If the strength of the letter predominates, they are likely to be strongly tinged with materialism, and yet, as 2 is inclined to be secretive and introspective, it is generally hard to detect its true feelings and sentiments. A 2 is apt to be very sensitive, and like all who live introspectively, intuitional. Even when in harmony, it is no uncommon thing to find a 2 possessing a melancholy turn of mind, and this tendency usually grows stronger in sympathy with the strength of discordant vibrations. In a "B" out of harmony, the tendency to secretiveness is not unlikely to exhibit itself in selfishness, untruthfulness, and dishonesty.

Additional Notes for "B"

If B is prominent in a name, as the initial letter and perhaps recurring several times, it will be found that the tendency of the person is to mold and form.

"B" as a Cornerstone: The B would give poise, sympathy and power to help others.

C or 3. Because "C" is a scattering letter it does not lend itself readily to work of accumulation. It is a spiritual letter and not in harmony with material things. As a result, they find it very hard to save money. Being a Universal Number, they are able to conduct several lines of effort at the same time. In fact, it fails to meet its highest possibilities if not provided with a multiplicity of interests, some of which should exert a wide influence. A 3 belongs to the intellectual vibrations, and frequently manifests itself in authorship, or in some other artistic profession. It makes the good talker, and would supply a ready spring of inspiration for the orator or promoter. It indicates the power to design, and would help the architect or any planner. It also insures executive ability, but it is not conducive to completion of plans once they have been made, especially when these plans are those of other persons. In opinions it is difficult for a 3 to be dogmatic about anything, and the more thoroughly a 3 comes into harmony, the more cheery and hopeful its disposition will become. A 3 in full harmony seldom knows what it means to worry, and this is particularly true when it is money matters that are concerned. A 3 is naturally generous; is a lover of the mysterious, and is apt to be honest and conscientious in all labors undertaken. In constructive work, however, is efforts tend towards the spiritual rather than the material. When out of harmony the scattering tendencies are emphasized. It then scatters everything – mentally, morally, physically, spiritually, materially. A 3 governs the liver, notably inharmonious vibrations often exhibit themselves in that organ. As it also affects the lungs and bronchial tubes, these parts of the body should be watched for any indication of discord.

Additional Notes for "C"

As a friendly letter in a name not holding a key position it would work towards expansion and wider influence when under that Cycle.

"C" as a Cornerstone: It is not in harmony with material things being a Living/Spiritual Letter. It is a scattering letter, and does not lend itself readily to the work of accumulation. As a result, C finds it difficult to save much money, and this is especially liable to be the case when the birth is 7. It is also both characteristic of both 7 and C that neither of them worry greatly over money losses. While their tendency is to make money easily, it is easily scattered. C stands for generosity, honesty and conscientiousness in any labor undertaken.

D or 4. As "D" is a letter of balance, 4 is a good number for an anchor; a strong force in the establishment of equilibrium. While it is capable of giving poise in conditions of nervousness, however, any inharmonious vibrations are apt to change its character conspicuously, bringing afflictions of every sort – losses in business, misfortunes in associations, and physically, diseases that are slow in response to treatment, particularly afflictions of the intestines. A 4 is naturally of sterling character; loyal to friends, and while not especially philanthropic, is usually generous to those who have any right to expect such generosity. A 4, however, generally insists that other people shall live up to its own particular ideal of right and justice, and it is extremely important that the 4 itself should obey the same law, for the slightest deviation for the path of sterling honesty, or the smallest tendency in the direction of intemperance, will change a noble character into one that is distinctively ignoble. A harmonious 4 usually adopts a business career, and not infrequently, is interested in mining affairs, or in realty transactions. Being an admirer of nature, and a home lover, it is no uncommon thing to find a 4 engaged in agricultural pursuits, and if the owner of the animals, a 4 is certain to make pets of them. A 4 should make every effort to avoid business relations with a 3. Its best associates are 2's, 8's, 11's, and 22's.

"D" as a Capstone: As a letter in the name that is both inharmonious to the Name Number and Birth Number, it would have the effect of producing poise and equilibrium.

E or 5. An "E" is possessed of a dual nature. Even when in harmony it is both beneficent and maleficent, although, under such favorable conditions, soul-racking regret and atonement follow all exhibitions of maleficence. Although a good number when in concord, it is apt to become a most dangerous one in discord, as many of its attractive qualities are easily reversed. When in harmony an "E" will probably be a social and entertaining person, although inclined to be more fond of dress and worldly things, than of the spiritual life. When such higher manifestations of character become possible, however, this 5 is both a philosophical and a peace-making element in society, but it must be remembered that, as 5 is usually of nervous temperament, becoming excited over little things, inclinations to impulsiveness, and sudden exhibitions of temper are apt to become a serious handicap when brought out by discordant conditions. Under inharmonious vibrations, therefore, these are the qualities to be feared, and the violence of the outbursts of temper will become greater if the 5 does not live true to the law of absolute temperance in all things. In fact, even in concordant conditions, a 5 frequently finds it difficult to maintain mental equilibrium. It is, therefore, absolutely essential that destructive impulses should never be obeyed, lest all kinds of troubles follow, including nervous disorders and indigestion; loss of friends, possibly through death, but more probably through estrangement, mishaps in business; loss of money, or similar complications. If under favorable conditions, however, the 5 possesses many attractive qualities. It is a business number, and is often interested in making money, especially by speculation. It also exhibits considerable mechanical ability, and if drawn towards spiritual things, may easily develop psychic powers. In every case, however, absolutely temperate habits must be maintained, or the soul will be wrecked. The most antagonistic vibrations to a 5 are 8 and 11.

Additional Notes for "E"

It stands for Great Material Prosperity and tireless industry.

They will subject the individual to such great suffering through malignant plots, the quarrels of subordinates, and gross ingratitude. If it follows an L in a name, which has the tendency to gather and retain material things bringing breadth and expansion, it will oppose these tendencies so what is accumulated in L will be disintegrate in E.

It inspires Love of humanity, leaning towards the mystic, and ease in the attraction of material comforts.

F or 6. In "F" we have another example of dual manifestations, another exhibition of opposing forces, strong to make or mar the character of the person possessing them. Under the effect of the higher vibrations, "F" is steadfast of purpose; firm in opinions, and with a loyalty to friends that remains unshaken, sometimes even when known to be wrong. This 6 is an idealist; a dreamer of dreams; one who can build air castles so realistically as to be able to live in them. Such a person usually works for others, rather than for self. A 6 is usually of artistic temperament; may be musical, and is intuitional in arriving at conclusions. As it is one of the Intellectual numbers, it is frequently found in the names of writers. Under discordant conditions, many of these qualities are changed. The imaginative quality that once jumped at conclusions now magnifies things unreasonably, borrowing trouble, and worrying over circumstances that exist largely, if not altogether in the mind of the individual. In other words, the power of intuition now becomes an unreasonable dread of impending calamity, and as the result, alternate attacks of mental exhilaration and depression usually follow. Under harmonious vibrations a 6 would make a good organizer, especially of social and ethical movements. For its own good, however, it must adhere closely to all the laws of the higher life; must abstain from alcoholic beverages, and must neither, speculate in stocks or gamble.

G or 7. As "G" is a letter of completion, those under its influence are usually able to carry out all their plans. They are also likely to be extremely methodical, both in act and in thought. Ordinarily hard to convince, owing to the innate necessity of studying every phase of a proposition before accepting it, any increase in vibratory strength would inspire the tendency to be strong-willed or even self-opinionated. As "G" always finds it hard to take advice, a 7 should be the director of men, not the occupant of a subordinate position. Many good lawyers and judges are 7's. It is also an inventive number, and usually attracts work connected with electrical science. In fact, the influences of "G" are exerted both upon the mental and the physical life. The 7 is an intellectual and philosophical number; if turned into psychic channels, it often inspires prophetic gifts. To the body it brings a strong reserve of physical strength, and when in full harmony, long and healthful life. Its effect upon the heart makes the bearer strong in passions and sentiments. When he likes, he loves; when he dislikes, he hates. There is seldom any halfway exhibitions of feeling. A 7 is a lover of literature, music, and art, and yet it frequently lacks the ability that makes the performer. The strongest opposition to "G" is found in the number 8, and yet, through a strange psychological paradox, a 7 usually exerts a strong attraction for an 11 or 22. But as such associations would have a most unfortunate effect upon all parties concerned, this influence should be strenuously resisted. The crimes of a discordant "G" are generally of a swindling nature.

Additional Notes for "G"

It gives a strongly philosophical turn to the mind. It would bring intensity to the power of completion; additional intellectuality, and a love for the study of the occult.

H or 8. The law of 8, in its manifestation of "H", is to create, to fulfill, to complete, it is usually sympathetic, often to the point of bearing the burdens of others, and yet, while it attracts the confidences of friends, it is so sufficient unto itself that it is seldom dependent upon other individuals for its happiness, finding easy contentment in solitude. While an 8 is liable to live introspectively, it usually tries to deal justly with all men, and, if under genuinely harmonious conditions, it will take great interest in work for humanity. When in discord, pronounced selfishness and extreme egotism may be developed. An "H" can frequently develop the powers of research, or invention, especially along mineral lines. If spiritually inclined, will probably take extreme positions in religious opinion, and yet, while not easily convinced of error, or quickly persuaded to change an opinion that has been accepted, such a person is seldom aggressive, or strong in contention, being more inclined to follow the line of least resistance. A lover of nature, music, and artistic things, an 8 might easily become a writer, an artist, or a musician. In spite of its generally happy and confident disposition, an "H", to be genuinely successful, must be in harmony in most of its vibrations, for even a slight discord has a tendency to change its beneficent characteristics. Thus, while it may be highly sympathetic with one in the Triad of 3-6-9, it is extremely antagonistic to a 5 or a 7. As it possesses a duality of forces, its activities should not be confined to a single interest.

Additional Notes for "H"

It tends to surgical operations.

The "H" would bring the ability to create or invent just like the "T". It brings the creative or inventive element into the name.

"H" as a Cornerstone: Since it is usually sympathetic, it would work in sympathy with the work of humanity of a 3, but it would also bring most inharmonious vibrations into the life.

I or 9. An "I" is largely a law unto itself. Being the Capstone of a Triad, or a completing number, its tendency is to finish whatever it undertakes. Being a strengthening force, however, it is likely to cause the repetition of work, making one do things over and over, until they meet the requirements of the ideal. These vibrations also manifest themselves in the matter of luck, an "I" having what are popularly termed "runs of luck", or several pieces of good or bad fortune in rotation. If one is under the direct influence of "I" the tendency is towards a change in both thought and things. If all conditions are harmonious, the change will be for the better, for higher intellectuality, more spirituality, and greater prosperity, if the efforts are along the line of best endeavor. As "I" is distinctively an individual letter, the person controlled by it is liable to be of strong will, chafing under dictation, and aggressively opposed to any attempt to put a limit upon his field of endeavor. Other persons may try to rule an "I", but they will find it difficult to keep such a personality under subjection. As "I", is an intellectual letter, and strongly original through its force of individuality, it indicates either literary or artistic ability – perhaps both. If it combines with the talking ability, its tendencies will be towards the lecture platform, rather than the pulpit. The attraction towards written or printed matter is so clearly defined, however, that an "I" without literary ability will ordinarily gravitate to clerical work. An "I" wants to hold a pen. It will create, if possible; if not, it will copy, but it must write – unless some discordant element is extraordinarily powerful. In fact, this trait of character is generally shown in infancy, for an "I" is usually a child who prefers to find amusement among books, and with paper and pencil, rather than in the out-of-door games that most children love. Accordingly, parents should approve of, rather than oppose these manifestations, for such a child, when intelligently directed, may be expected to develop marked ability in literary or artistic pursuits. When "I" is out of harmony its effect is liable to be anything but advantageous. As it affects the nervous direction. Extreme nervousness may develop; extreme conditions of life may follow, and apparently insurmountable obstacles may arise to prevent the successful culmination of plans. An "I" under strong discord is likely to be extremely forgetful; will do things over and over unnecessarily, and the frequent repetitions of ill luck will not improbably end in despondency.

Additional Notes for "I"

If I is prominent in a name, as the initial letter and perhaps recurring several times, it will be found that there will be the quickness of comprehension which is in a way a revelation, and there will also be a sense of justice and the power to judge.

"I" as a Keystone: When inharmonious to the Birth Number it brings separation from friends, material losses, and nervous afflictions.

J or 10. The "J" or 10, maintains the predominating characteristics of 1, but in more intense vibration. As "J" is the stronger letter – stronger both in material and spiritual things – it helps to carry out the plans of "A". Moreover, "J" has higher aspirations, aspirations that tend to develop its powers in the direction of deeper things. Like "A", "J" is a designer, an architect, a planner, but upon a higher plane. Still, to be successful, "J" must direct, not obey, and for this the number has been given more than a proportionate share of executive ability. A "J" also stands for change – new thoughts, new things. Thus, under a harmonious Cycle of "J" important business changes may be made without hesitation. A "J" is generally honest, just, and benevolent, but he requires that others shall conform to his own ideals of integrity and righteousness. Accordingly, "J" must be true to the purity of his life motives, for any discord in this direction will result in serious mental, if not physical suffering.

K or 20. A "K" resembles "B", except that its vibrations are much stronger. In fact, it is a letter of extremes – extremes in mental conditions, extremes in fortune, extremes of health, extremes of spirituality. Intensity of nature almost invariable controls a "K". It knows no twilight. It recognizes no half-hearted measures. If it is not happy, it is miserable. If it is not good, it is evil. There are no possible heights of attainment to which it cannot reach; no depths of iniquity to which it cannot descend. As the result, one who comes under the control of this letter cannot afford to offend against any law – either the law of man or the law of God. He must think pure thoughts. He must be just and honest in all his dealings with men, for though, of strong will, the penalties that will be certain to follow any violation of the law of love cannot be evaded. When under free rein, "K" indicates versatility, and capability in many fields of endeavor. If restrained, however, it stands for small attainment. A "K", for self preservation, should neither gamble not drink intoxicating liquors.

L or 30. "L" has many of the spiritual characteristics of "C", but in the material sense, there is a difference, for while "C" scatters, "L" not only gathers, but retains a reasonable portions of the things that it accumulates. Also, in other respects it holds the power of bringing to completion the things that are merely under process of organization in "C". While "L" is quite as philanthropic as "C", its generosity is exhibited in a wiser form. It gives generously, but justly, and for all that it does, it asks appreciation, often losing its desire to give to the degree that such recognition is withheld. To a similar extent, "L" strives persistently to gather the fruits of its labors, and finds its greatest inspiration in a plentiful harvest. "C" will plant without hope of reward in this life, "L" insists upon gathering. At the same time, "L" generally uses its forces wisely. It is a letter that belongs to a leader of men; to persons of executive ability, and considerable intellectuality. An "L" often surpasses in art, music, or literature. Under harmonious conditions it also may attain to high spiritual powers. Even when in discord, it has no evil attributes of character, although it may effect the health through the lungs, or breath.

Additional Notes for "L"

It brings the tendency towards breadth and expansion in many directions, executive ability and power in leadership. The tendency of L is to gather and retain material things and it would also help to retain that which is accumulated. It intensifies the executive ability; instills the wisdom that uses forces wisely, and being a Living/Spiritual Letter, neutralizes the effects of the discordant letter that follows. In a name where it precedes an E, this tendency would be opposed.

M or 40. The "M" spiritualizes the attributes of "D", being the strongest vibration in the Triad of 2-4-8. It is so full of life, strength, and integrity that it is both a creative and a productive number. It deals justly with everybody, but while firm for the right, it will not become aggressive under wrong. In other words, instead of fighting, a 40 will urge arbitration as a means of adjusting difficulties. As the result, "M" cannot be a leader. It will serve faithfully and honestly, but its greatest success comes from executing plans made by others. It sometimes shows some originality, especially when it becomes a worker of the soil, but is strongest quality is spirituality. Under proper vibrations it may develop remarkable psychic gifts, and there is not letter that will bear a cross so bravely, or with so little complaint. Thus, when out of harmony, "M" will bring many burdens into the life.

Additional Notes for "M"

As a friendly letter in a name, it would exert a powerful effect in the establishment of a suitable environment for work.

"M" as a Capstone: "M" is a burden bearer.

N or 50. "N" is not a good letter, although, when in harmony, and kept under absolute control, it frequently develops many praiseworthy traits. There is nothing stable about "N" and, however harmonized, it is always negative. It incites jealousy, envy, and much unkindness. It is often malicious, holding fast to sentiments of spite and feelings of hatred. Being in every sense a material letter, "N" in full harmony should find little trouble in accumulating a fortune, although it may not be extremely particular as to the methods it adopts in getting this money. It is a marrying letter, but, as its dominion is transient, domestic happiness is scarcely likely to follow. As "N" is a mental letter, a person under its influence often makes a good teacher. In fact, association with children is one of the best avenues of escape for the surplus energies of "N". Philanthropic pursuits is another. Moreover, as "N" has its physical manifestations through the circulation of the blood, inharmonious vibrations are liable to extend to any portion of the body, resulting in nervousness and blood poisons, like those of rheumatism, etc. Many of these natural characteristics may be neutralized by proper arrangement of harmonious influences.

Additional Notes for "N"

It tends to surgical operations. It stands for great material prosperity along with tireless industry.

If N is prominent in a name, as the initial letter and perhaps recurring several times, it will be found that whatever is achieved, affliction in some form accompanies it.

"N" as a Cornerstone: If inharmonious to the Birth Number and as a material letter and in direction opposition to a 2 through an 11 Birth Number, it would carry the undercurrent of its most undesirable qualities, including jealousy, hatred, spite, intrigue, etc.

O or 60. "O" possesses practically all of the good and evil qualities of "F". In many instances it even accentuates them. Thus, it displays more genius for order; it is more systematic; more intellectual; more firmly set in opinions, and more intuitional. "F" frequently leaves work uncompleted; "O" persists in finishing all that it undertakes, for it is not easy to make an "O" acknowledge defeat. Although possessed of little originality, "O" makes a good imitator, and while such a person may write, or display artistic, or musical ability, it will be difficult for him to become great in any of these pursuits. In religious thought "O" is more liberal than "F".

Additional Notes for "O"

The "O" would bring steadfastness and intellectual strength and would give any steadying influence to any letters that would indicate high imagination or inventive abilities.

If "O" is a friendly letter in a name it would bring steadfastness, loyalty to friends, and literary ability. It tends to literary work.

P or 70. "P" intensifies the characteristics of "G", finishing what "G" begins and leaves unfinished. Occupying a higher spiritual plane than "G", it has stronger individuality, and is usually distinctively original, sometimes to the point of eccentricity. "P" also aspires to lead, and is not only impatient of restrictions, but must be allowed free rein, under penalty of being thrown out of equilibrium if restrained. As "P" is an intellectual letter, it is often productive of excellent literary or artistic work. It may even create the musician; possibly, the vocalist. Although honest and upright in its inclinations, it is in danger of missing opportunities by reason of its desire to study every phase of each proposition considered. The remedy is to act more impulsively by placing more dependence upon intuition. Under harmonious conditions, a "P" might make a political former, a philosopher, or an organizer. In every case, however, such an individual must be careful not to overstep the bounds of love and equity, for all his deeds, whether good or evil, are certain to come back to bless or confound him. By observing proper precautions, a "P" should live a long and useful life.

Additional Notes for "P"

The "P" in a name would make one impatient at restriction, and would give aspirations to leadership, and originality, even to eccentricity.

Q or 80. "Q" is a stronger manifestation of the qualities displayed by "H". It shows more originality; has more intensity of feeling; greater aspirations towards leadership. It is an intellectual letter, often showing genius for philosophy, or scientific research. Is strong in inductive reasoning, and good in arranging a convincing argument. If satisfied that he has a mission to perform, such a person is not easily dominated, but he will always be most successful when supplied with two channels of expression. In discord, a "Q" might become extremely unscrupulous (lack of morals, no conscience, no respect for law).

R or 90. "R" holds all the possibilities of "I", the 9 of single vibration, except that it represents the bright side of the number. It is more spiritual than "I", "R" being a living letter, and is not so subject to the loss of things loved. As "R" is an intellectual letter, it belongs to the name of one who is interested in writing, or printing; as it is a completing letter, its occurrence in a name indicates that this Cycle will be the best period for development. Thus, should one aspire to progress towards nobler, or higher effort, such a Cycle is the most promising time in which to shape the life in the desired direction, as "R" holds the power to bring out the greatest human possibilities. When in harmony, therefore, "R" is extremely beneficent. When out of harmony, however, it induces losses – loss of money, loss of health, loss of friends, loss of articles valued, etc.

Additional Notes for "R"

It stands for realization as a completing letter.

When Harmonious it tends to literary work.

Be careful to see that "R" is followed by a favorable letter. If under full harmony, "R" is beneficent, and will bring beneficial changes. Why? Maybe because "R" is "9" and this is the number of change.

"R" as a Cornerstone: "R" indicates the writer; the orator: the man with a message, and the power to express it. As a Living/Spiritual letter it influences the entire name. In the example given it is out of harmony with the Birth Number, but yet it still has these qualities to offer. Maybe because it was in harmony with the Name Number in the example given.

"R" as a Keystone: All literary aspirations would be intensified, and literary labors would be brought to completion. It would also have a marked changed in other things – in modes of thought, in associations, and in environment.

S or 100. "S" is another architectural letter, but intensified in its spirituality. When harmonious, it is beneficent; when inharmonious, disastrous, deadly. It makes or mars, but usually strikes extremes. When inharmonious conditions exist, the effect may possibly be seen through troubles with the kidneys. To live successfully under "S" it is not sufficient that all numerical forces should vibrate concordantly. Besides the harmony of numbers, there must be harmony of life. In other words, it is the law that "S" must constantly hold an attitude of spiritual communion with all creation and all creatures – assuming a position of love, peace, and benefaction towards all things, not only in word and deed, but in thought as well.

Additional Notes for "S"

It stands for the beginning of new things. To live the Cycle of "S" harmoniously, one must assume the position of love, peace and benefaction towards all things.

"S" as a Capstone: It is more intense than 1 in its degree of spirituality.

T or 200. "T" is another dual letter that, while rich in individuality, knows no middle ground. It is righteous, or the contrary; will save, or slay; will build up, or break down. A "T" is usually dictatorial, and will seek to control every individual who comes within its influence. It is the natural molder, and is unhappy if it cannot shape things to its liking. As "T" is also the symbol of the law of divine compensation, it demands the privilege of reaping when it has sown. To enjoy success under "T" one must attain to the mastery of self, for, even when in perfect harmony, a "T" must be a master of self-control that the maleficent influences of the letter may have no opportunity to dominate.

Additional Notes for "T"

As a natural molder and unhappy if it cannot shape things to its liking, the "T" would bring the ability to create or invent just like the H. The number 2 is a Cornerstone in the 2-4-8 Triad and is natural for initiating, beginning, creating, or inventing.

"T" as a Cornerstone: "T" would have the effect of emphasizing the dictatorial side of nature and would impel the person influenced by it to strive to dominate every situation.

U or 300. The "U" manifests many of the qualities of "C", but, being more spiritual in its operation, it emphasizes them. Thus, "U" will be quite tenacious in holding the things that it accumulates, showing even more tenacity in this regard that "L" exhibits. "U" has the universal spirit of both "C" and "L", but as it is more inclined to bind, it is more hopeful in temperament, less easily discouraged, less liable to despondency. When out of harmony, however, "U" becomes extremely selfish, even to the point of miserliness.

Additional Notes for "U"

When in harmony with the name, not necessarily the Birth Number, it intensifies all the characteristics of the Name Number.

V or 400. A "V" combines the qualities of "M" and "Q". It is a home-loving force, with strong disinclination to travel. It is fixed in its opinions; firm in its friendships, and square in its dealings with men. Though a strong lover of nature, a "V" would find little pleasure in tilling the soil. It is more interested in things that appear above ground. Thus, a "V" is tinged with the artistic, it would make the successful landscape gardener, or florist, the tendencies leading towards experimentation through grafting, etc. Like many other spiritual letters, "V" has a duality of forces. In one phase of manifestation it is the personification of equilibrium, or practical things. In its other nature, it is a dweller in two worlds; a dreamer; a castle-builder; the judge who delves deeply in search of the intention behind the deed, in the belief that it is the motive more than the act that counts. If not harmonious, however, "V" may become very impractical.

W or 500. "W" is another regenerative letter, and is strongly beneficent when its spiritual law is comprehended and lived both in spirit and letter. It is a letter of aspiration, and yet such aspirations cannot be realized if faith does not govern. A "W" must believe in the means before he can use it to attain an end. "W" is a completing letter, and is the spiritualization of "E" and "N". To live this letter advantageously, one must know and follow the divine law of love and justice. When out of harmony, "W" frequently develops tendencies to secretiveness, selfishness, dishonesty, etc.

Additional Notes for "W"

It stands for Great Material Prosperity and tireless industry.

X or 600. "X" is the spiritual completion of "F" and "O", and neutralizes their material qualities. Their maleficent forces are at last overcome, and their beneficent promises are realized. At the same time "X" performs a double office. It is the Roman numeral representing the number 10, and its influence in the life of the individual corresponds closely to its effect in Roman notation. Thus, when placed before other letters, it diminishes their force, as when:

$$X (10) \text{ and } L (50) = 40$$

When placed after a letter, it increases, or adds its own force to that already exerted, as when:

$$L (50) \text{ and } X (10) = 60$$

Next to "E" and "N", "X" is the greatest tipler, and inharmonious vibrations may not improbably show themselves in that direction. Such discords may also arouse unreliable, or erratic tendencies.

Y or 700. "Y" is a letter of promise, but its fulfillment is often long deferred. It is a patient letter, as the knowledge that one may have long to wait induces patience. Another tendency of the letter is to help in upbuilding the memory. Under favorable conditions a "Y" may be blessed with psychic powers. When in proper concord, or under its Cycle, it might create a skillful musician, painter, jeweler, silversmith, or high-grade mechanic. Its successes, however, would be based more upon the mechanical side, than upon the spiritual, or artistic plane. When out of harmony, "Y" might tend strongly towards egotism – the uplifting and worship of the individual "I" – or it might become easy-going to the point of laziness.

Z or 800. This letter holds all the qualities of "H" and "Q", but intensified spiritually. It opens the door to the knowledge of higher things. It creates a love for the mysterious and fosters a desire to study the occult, or psychic. It does not aid in the work of creating. It does not help the inventor. It explores; it discovers; it investigates – new things, new lands, new remedies. A person controlled by the forces of "Z" might make a good chemist, a persevering psychologist, or a painstaking student in some other experimental field. When out of harmony, "Z" is not good for health.

ADDITIONAL LETTER CLASSIFICATIONS

In addition to the above descriptions, there are 4 more letter classifications that are pertinent to the interpretations that are to follow. Clement goes on to say that

> "In ascertaining the effect of the name upon the individual life, every letter has its value in pointing the course of the harmonious or inharmonious vibrations. At the same time, there are certain letters that exert a stronger force than others, the most important being classified as Living or Spiritual Letters, Individualized Letters, Universal Letters, and Material Letters. Thus: the Living, or Spiritual Letters, which vibrate with the greatest intensity through the entire name are "C", "G", "H", "I', "L", "M", "R", "U", and "V"."

> These letters must be lived on the side of faith, hope, and truth because they are subject to extreme conditions, and under less spiritual manifestations they will tend to mould the life to fit the other extremity, guiding the soul into absolutely contrary channels. Such letters stand out resplendently in any name if lived conscientiously."

The Material Letters are "J", "K", "L", "M", "N", "O", "P", "Q", and "R". They bring the power to think material thoughts and accumulate material things. Notice that these letters all correspond to the Letters of double vibration and thus, to the Keystone. Recall that the Keystone bears the weight of the arch and should therefore be a strong Material Letter. He points out that some of these letters are included in both classes – Spiritual & Material, and that this indicates that while their strongest influence is felt from the Spiritual side, they are also affected by Material vibrations, just as people of high spiritual nature are not infrequently blessed with almost perfect physical health and a large share of worldly goods. The letters that belong to both categories are "L", "M", and "R". The Material Letters would bring inflexibility of purpose, and the compelling force that bends others to one's will. Thus, an abundance of Material Letters in the name would make one of an unmovable and of a fixed-will.

The Universal Letters are "C", "I", "L", "R", and "U"." Notice that these are the letters whose numerical equivalents are "3" and "9". Since they are all a part of the Spiritual classification of letters, they are said to be strongly in sympathy with the spiritual vibrations, and they are the letters that will strive most persistently to perform universal work. In addition, having a numerical value of either "3" or "9", they are the Cornerstone and Capstones of the 3,6,9 Triad. Thus, they are of either an initiating or completing force and vibrate as the most influential letters of this Triad in the name.

The Individualized Letters are the "K", "P", "Q", "S", "T", "Y", and "Z"." He says that they owe their name to the fact that they represent so strong a force that they frequently shine both ways, sometimes vibrating in three cycles." I assume that based on this statement, the author is referring to their influence with respect to the cycles, which we haven't gotten to just yet. Take note of the fact the numerical equivalent of these numbers is 2, 7, 8, 1, 2, 7, 8, where S is the only one in the triple vibration. These letters are also all Cornerstones or Capstones to their respective Triads.

> "In reading a name, the most successful method is to commence by reading the Birth Number. Follow by reading the Name Number, and compare the Triads, noting the position that they occupy in their relation to one an-

other. Study the effect of the Cornerstone upon the name, then consider the influence of the Keystone, if there should be one, and do not neglect the Capstone."

Next, the work to be done is to simply note whether the Cornerstone, Keystone, and Capstone is in harmony with the Birth Number. If it is in harmony, then it will influence the individual with its beneficial vibrations under the description given for that letter. If it is in discord, then it will influence the individual with its negative vibrations as given for that letter. The force of those vibrations is determined by whether it is in the ones, tens, or hundreds place as given. In addition to these, you can analyze every letter in the name in the same manner, and also note the occurrence of certain letters in a name, and how they might intensify their influence on the individual for good or for bad.

Last, but not least, when the numbers in a name are not in harmony with the Birth Number, they still may be in sympathy or share similar attributes so as not to be all bad. They may in fact work together quite well. This is when those additional classifications come in handy to see if the letters are in the same category. With this in mind, we will look at some examples in the next chapter, and then look at how Gann used this information in his 1919 article.

5

Character Analysis

In his book, Clement provides an example of an individual named Alice Ames who was born on the 20th of July. Although the last name was given, he only analyzes the first name in order to put more emphasis on teaching the method. July 20th equates to a Birth Number of "2", and this belongs to the 2, 4, 8 Triad. The Name Number is calculated as follows:

```
A   L   I   C   E
1   3   9   3   5   =  21  =  3
```

First, we take note of the fact that the Name Number "3" is in discord with the Birth Number "2". Next, we look at the Stones. The Cornerstone "A", has a numerical value of 1. The Keystone is "I", which has a numerical value of "9", and the Capstone is "E", which has a numerical value of "5". None of these numbers are in harmony with the Birth Number, which is a "2". In fact, none of the letters in the name are in harmony with the Birth Number.

Taking the above into consideration, Clement interprets the combination by first commenting on the Cornerstone saying,

> "this would lead one to begin many things, but there are no vibrations in the name that would help such a person finish them. The Keystone "I", would bring separation from friends, material losses, and nervous afflictions. The "C", which follows "I", would continue to scatter everything that 2 – the Birth Number – could gather."

If you refer back to the descriptions for each of the letters that he mentions and note their inharmonious influences, you will see why Clement has made these statements. For example, under the Letter "A" there is a section at the end where it says,

> "An "A" out of harmony would be obstinate and headstrong. The tendency to "begin" things would still exist, but the power to "finish" would be weakened to correspond to the extent of vibratory discord."

The Cornerstone "A" is the natural Cornerstone for the 1-5-7 Triad, and needs a Letter with a numerical value of "7", which is the Capstone or completing force, in order to finish what is began. Under the Letter "I" it says,

> "When "I" is out of harmony its effect is liable to be anything but advantageous. As it affects the nervous organism, discord is apt to be felt in that direction. Extreme nervousness may develop . . ."

This accounts for him saying that there could be nervous afflictions. As for the separation from friends & material losses, you will find that under the section for the letter "E", which is the Capstone in the name. It also indicates nervous disorders, along with loss of friends, mishaps in business, and loss of money. Under the description for "C", it tells you quite plainly that it is a scattering letter as it does not lend itself readily to the work of accumulation. Now that we have the procedure, let's see if we can use this same method to decipher some of the things Gann says in his 1919 article.

In the *Milwaukee Sentinel* Magazine article published in 1919, which you have read in its entirety in the second chapter, we will focus only on the statements concerning the divination of the name as it pertains to Wilhelm Hohenzollern. We will look at how he may have forecasted specific dates later in the book. Now, in the beginning of

CHARACTER ANALYSIS

the article, Gann makes some specific statements and characterizations about Wilhelm Hohenzollern based on his associated names. They include the given name, his mother's maiden name, and his surname, which he inherited from his father. In relation to these names, Gann wrote as follows:

> "Wilhelm Hohenzollern, the infamous imperial scoundrel, whose crimes against women and children have debauched and shocked the civilized world and caused him to be the most hated and despised man in history, was born January 27, 1859. His mother, Princess Victoria Adelaide, Mary Louisa Wettin, was born Nov 21, 1840.
>
> A study of the mother's maiden name, which always reveals the secret nature and future destiny of the male child more than the father's name, indicates the remarkable events in the Kaiser's life. Her name shows that the husband lacked love and sympathy for her, which is fully manifested in the depraved feelings and unsympathetic nature of her son. The name Hohenzollern shows that he would inherit from his father an unbalanced mind; that he would be an egotist, a braggart and a selfish coward. . .
>
> His name and numbers indicated that he would inherit a throne, property and wealth and then lose them all in his own acts. His numbers reveal the fact that all vain hopes would be defeated in the end.
>
> The letter W is a twin letter or a letter with a dual nature. While it is one of justice and fairness, when afflicted it becomes one of the most selfish and debased influences. The letter N is the most powerful letter for producing wealth and fame, especially when the surname begins with W and ends with N. It overcomes all obstacles and wins in the end. . . When H is the initial letter, it attempts to create position of wealth and power through destruction."

This is a mouthful, so let's start dissecting this bit by bit to see if we can see how he came to these conclusions using information obtained from Clement's book.

First off, Gann provides us with Wilhelm's birthdate from which the Birth Number is 9, since he was born on the 27th of the month and 2 + 7 = 9. This means that his concord is the 3, 6, 9 Triad. The Name number breaks down as follows:

```
W   I   L   H   E   L   M
5   9   3   8   5   3   4   =  37  =  10  =  1
```

We note that the 1 is not in harmony with the 3,6,9 Triad. Next, we note the key positions in the name Wilhelm and any letters that occur more than once, which are as follows:

Cornerstone:	W	(Causes Discord)
Keystone:	H	(Causes Discord)
Capstone:	M	(Causes Discord)
Repeating Letters:	L	(Causes Harmony)

Now that we have the components of the given name, let's look at the next influence, which is the mother's maiden name. As a side note, as far as I could find in my research, this is unique to Gann with respect to the study of numbers in the era after 1902. Aso-Neith nor Lou Clement never mentions the use of the mother's maiden name in divination. L. Dow Balliett briefly mentions the use of the mother's maiden name in her 1905 book entitled, *How to Attain Success Through the Strength of Vibration: A System of Numbers as Taught by Pythagoras*, but does not provide any examples on how to utilize the information. If I may quote from the version I have, published by Sun Publishing Company with a copyright date of 1983, on page 13 she writes,

"If Mother's maiden name added weakens the vibration of baptismal name,
its weakness must rather be met and overcome than held in abeyance."

This is it, and as far as I can tell, it is never mentioned in subsequent works. The only other person who utilizes the mother's maiden name after 1902 in divining the name is Veolita Parke Boyle in her book entitled, *Fundamental Principles of Yi-King, Tao: The Cabbalas of Egypt and the Hebrews* published in 1929.

If I may add, I find this to be a very unique and interesting system. There are additional books, pamphlets, etc. that go with the above quoted book, and I have managed to acquire all of them, even the author's original typed manuscript for the book along with some personal notes, which contains material that has never been in print as far

CHARACTER ANALYSIS

as I know. It is well worth taking a look at. The only other systems where the Mother's name played a role in divination for an individual is in Medieval Europe, where they were most likely influenced by ancient Greek, Indian, and Arabic sources. Now to continue, Wilhelm's mother's maiden name is as follows:

W E T T I N
5 5 2 2 9 5 = 28 = 10 = 1

Cornerstone:	W	(Causes Discord)
Keystone:		(No Keystone)
Capstone:	N	(Causes Discord)
Repeating Letters:	T	(Causes Discord)

Last, the surname, which is inherited from the father is:

H O H E N Z O L L E R N
8 6 8 5 5 8 6 3 3 5 9 5 = 71 = 8

Cornerstone:	H	(Causes Discord)
Keystone:		(No Keystone)
Capstone:	N	(Causes Discord)
Repeating Letters:	H, O, E, N, L	(The O & L are in Concord/Harmony)

With the details of these three names and the day of birth (27th), let's analyze the first part of the article where Gann says,

> "A study of the mother's maiden name, which always reveals the secret nature and future destiny of the male child more than the father's name, indicates the remarkable events in the Kaiser's life. Her name shows that the husband lacked love and sympathy for her, which is fully manifested in the depraved feelings and unsympathetic nature of her son."

Personally, this passage is the most difficult to decipher using Clement's letter descriptions. However, note the fact that the name Wettin has two T's, which indicates they have a strong influence in the name because they appear more than once. Under the description for the letter "T", Clement says,

> ""T" is another dual letter, that, while rich in individuality, knows no middle ground. It is righteous, or the contrary; will save, or slay; will upbuild, or break down. A "T" is usually dictatorial, and will seek to control every individual who comes within its influence. It is the natural moulder, and is unhappy if it cannot shape things to its liking."

This is the very definition of one who is unsympathetic. They don't how the other person feels. It has to be their way or no way at all. When you combine this with the fact that the letter is not in harmony with the Birth Number, it brings out the negative tendencies to a higher degree than in someone who has only one "T", which is not in any of the key positions. Thus, when negative, the "T" or "2" is unsympathetic, intolerant, bigoted and narrow-minded. It knows no middle ground. It will not give in or bend. These are double influences in the name Wettin.

Moving on, we find that Gann uses the words "depraved feelings" in addition to "unsympathetic" to describe Wilhelm. Depraved means corrupt, wicked, or perverted. Synonyms are evil, sinful, debased, and degenerate. This is brought out by the Keystone, which is "W". Under this letter, Clement says,

> "When out of harmony, "W" frequently develops tendencies to . . . dishonesty, etc."

The last letter to consider is the Capstone, which is "N" where Clement says,

> "It incites jealousy, envy, and much unkindness. It is often malicious, holding fast to sentiments of spite and feelings of hatred."

All of the key positions and letters with more than one occurrence are out of harmony and influence his characteristics and tendencies in a negative manner. When you consider that the Keystone and Capstone are in harmony with each other, it brings this out even more, not withstanding that these letters are also in harmony with the Name Number.

In the next sentence, Gann talks about the influence of the father's name.

> "The name Hohenzollern shows that he would inherit from his father an unbalanced mind; that he would be an egotist, a braggart and a selfish coward. . ."

CHARACTER ANALYSIS

The Cornerstone is "H". Under this letter in Clement's book it says,

> "When in discord, pronounced selfishness and extreme egotism may be developed."

This is further accentuated in this name because the letter occurs twice in the name. More importantly, closely compare what Gann says to the description in Clement's book. You see that it is a near perfect match with respect to the ego and selfishness. The other letter that is repeated twice is the "E", and it has good support because of the presence of "N", which also appears twice in the name and serves as the Capstone. In Clement's book on page 67 under the description for "E", it says,

> ". . . 5 is usually of nervous temperament, becoming excited over little things, inclinations to impulsiveness, and sudden exhibitions of temper are apt to become a serious handicap when brought out by discordant conditions. Under inharmonious vibrations, therefore, these are the qualities to be feared . . . even under concordant conditions, a 5 frequently finds it difficult to maintain proper mental equilibrium."

Here, we find the reason for Gann saying that Wilhelm inherits an unbalanced mind from his father. In addition to this, The Capstone "N", which is also a 5, also adds to this concept. On page 81 of Clement's book under the letter "N", he says,

> "There is nothing stable about "N" and however harmonized, it is always negative."

This further adds to the instability & unstableness that is described by Gann as an unbalanced mind. So in his father's name, we have two E's and two N's, with one N serving as the important Capstone, and they are all discordant. Thus, we see Gann's reasons for making these statements in the 1919 article are fully explained based on the descriptions in Clement's book.

Moving on, and skipping over the section on the given name, later in the passage Gann says,

> "The letter W is a twin letter or a letter with a dual nature. While it is one of justice and fairness, when afflicted it becomes one of the most selfish

and debased influences. The letter N is the most powerful letter for producing wealth and fame, especially when the surname begins with W and ends with N. It overcomes all obstacles and wins in the end. . . When H is the initial letter, it attempts to create position of wealth and power through destruction."

If you refer to the bottom of page 89 in Clement's book or under the description for this letter in the third chapter, you will find the following statement,

> "To live this letter advantageously, one must know and follow the divine law of love and justice. When out of harmony, "W" frequently develops tendencies to secretiveness, selfishness, dishonesty, etc."

Gann is saying the exact same thing, but its just phrased in a different way. This is the dual nature of the letter. It can lean to justice and fairness, but under discordant conditions it leans to the negative tendencies. So the "W", which serves as the Cornerstone in not only his given name, but in that of his mother's maiden name, which is also in discord with his Birth Number, will cause tendencies towards selfishness, dishonesty, etc.

Continuing with this passage where he speaks about the "W", he moves on to the letter "N". He says,

> "The letter N is the most powerful letter for producing wealth and fame, especially when the surname begins with W and ends with N."

In Clement's book on page 81 or under the description for the Letter "N", it says,

> "Being in every sense a material letter, "N" in full harmony should find little trouble in accumulating a fortune, although it may not be extremely particular as to the methods it adopts in getting this money."

Once again, we find congruence between Gann and Clement. We have the "W", "N", letter combination in Wilhelm's mother's name, which serves as the Cornerstone & Capstone in that name. Continuing with the passage, Gann says that when the "H" is the initial letter as opposed to "W", as in his father's name, it attempts to create wealth through destruction. Under the "H" we find the following,

CHARACTER ANALYSIS

"The law of 8, in its manifestation of "H", is to create, to fulfill, to complete."

With its natural tendency to want to create, and serving as the initial Letter or Cornerstone in his father's name, we see why Gann says that it will attempt to create wealth, but through destruction, which the latter is characteristic of the last letter, "N", of which I have already quoted above. The "N" should find little trouble in accumulating a fortune, although it may not be extremely particular as to the methods in getting it. Thus, through underhanded means due to the discord. This is how the Cornerstone and Keystone are working together.

Last, but not least, we come to the given name. Gann says,

"His name and numbers indicated that he would inherit a throne, property and wealth and then lose them all in his own acts. His numbers reveal the fact that all vain hopes would be defeated in the end."

The first thing to point out are the double L's in the name and couple this with the fact that they are in harmony with his Birth Number. Clement says on page 78 under the letter "L",

"[it] has many of the spiritual characteristics of "C", but, in the material sense, there is a difference, for, while "C" scatters, "L" not only gathers, but retains a reasonable portion of the things that it accumulates."

It therefore indicates a strong ability to accumulate material things such as property, wealth, etc., and given his family environment, a good reason to say that he would inherit a throne, property, and wealth. Take note of the fact that these are the only letters that repeat in his name so they are a strong force for good. On the other hand, as for the statement that he would lose them all in his own acts, this is indicated by the Cornerstone, Keystone, and Capstone.

The "W" as his Cornerstone in the given name has been talked about extensively under his mother's name. We read that one must know and follow the divine law of love and justice to live this letter advantageously. If not, it develops selfish tendencies. Now consider this in relationship to his Keystone, which is the letter "H". Under this letter, Clement says,

> "When in discord, pronounced selfishness and extreme egotism may be developed."

Here we find that although the Cornerstone "5" and Keystone "8" are not in the same concord, they are sympathetic with each other in their tendencies towards selfishness. In addition, since they are not in harmony with the Birth Number, they will bring out all the negative tendencies. This is why Gann said that all "vain", hence, "selfish" hopes would be defeated in the end. His own destructive impulses, his own acts, would be his undoing in the end. These vibrate very strongly throughout his given name. The "M", which serves as the Capstone of his give name has this to say:

> " . . . when out of harmony. "M" will bring many burdens into the life."

Thus, if we combine the influence of these key letters as if to form a sentence, we can say that his attempts to create through selfish, dishonest means, will in turn bring many burdens into his life.

As you can see, I am in no way grasping at straws in the analysis presented thus far. What Gann says about each of the names closely matches the letter descriptions in Clement's book. After putting together this information some time ago, I had no doubt in my mind that Gann was using these descriptions to divine the name. So if there was any question as to what system of numerology he was using in the article, this in my opinion answers it.

In addition, I have in no way fully explained all of the nuances in Clement's book. The goal here was to simply show that it is the basis for Gann's method of divination of the name in the 1919 article. For a more detailed and thorough explanation of the system, I refer you to his work directly and the articles on Aso-Neith.

As this concludes the character analysis portion of the article, we will now move on to analyzing the statements in the article on good and evil periods. However, before we go down that road, we need to understand how to forecast per the Aso-Neith system in order to see if this is how Gann forecasted the good and evil periods in the article.

6

Forecasting Per The Aso-Neith System

In Luo Clement's book on page 33, there is a section on Fortunate Days, Months, and Years. He writes,

"Another influence of the Triads that may be turned to considerable advantage in all the affairs of life may be found in their effect upon the months and the days of the month, for there are harmonious and inharmonious, or fortunate and unfortunate days, just as there are numbers that are in concord and numbers that are in discord with the particular vibration in which we have our being."

The following table is a list of the Harmonious months and days for each Triad.

HARMONIOUS MONTHS   **HARMONIOUS DAYS**

1st	1, 5, 7	Jan, May, Jul, Oct	1, 5, 7, 10, 14, 16, 19, 23, 25, 28
2nd	2, 4, 8	Feb, Apr, Aug, Nov	2, 4, 8, 11, 13, 17, 20, 22, 26, 29, 31
3rd	3, 6, 9	Mar, Jun, Sep, Dec	3, 6, 9, 12, 15, 18, 21, 24, 27, 30

Notice that if your harmonious Triad is 1-5-7, then your harmonious months are the 1st, 5th, 7th, & 10th months of the year, which are those very same numbers. Likewise, the

W.D. GANN: DIVINATION BY MATHEMATICS

days of the months that are harmonious will be those that when reduced through further addition are equal to the numbers of the Triad. For example, the 14th day of the month further reduces to 5 through the addition of 1 + 4. It is as simple as that.

Clement tells us that when beginning new things or undertaking important enterprises, we must be careful to bring our material interests into harmonious vibration with our fortunate days, months, and years. He then goes on to say that in the effect, the days exert greater force than the months, and the months are more important than the years, and that the years influence general conditions more than particular events.

To find the fortunate years for an individual, Clement tells us that those years that can be divided by the Birth Number are fortunate, and those that are not so divisible are unfortunate. Then, he gives an example of the year 1908, and points out that it can be divided by any number in the 3-6-9 Triad, and is therefore harmonious to a person in this Triad. Unfortunately, this is all he has to say about unfortunate years. Personally, I have concerns about this method because it doesn't make much sense when you consider that for a person born on the 1st of the month, every year would be harmonious because every year would be divisible by 1. For now, we will leave it as taught to us by Clement and move on to the next topic, which is the cycles.

CYCLES

Under the section entitled "Cycles" on page 49 of his book, Clement writes,

"A Cycle, in the application of the Science of Numbers, is a period of nine years, and the effect of the Cycle upon the life of the individual is to make the characteristics of each letter of the name assert the greatest degree of influence during the period of nine years in which it is in force."

Then he provides an example using the name "John". The first letter "J", would have an influence during the first 9 years of John's life, that is, from the beginning to the end of the 9th year, when John would turn 9 years old. Following the "J", the characteristics of the letter "O" would assert themselves from the beginning of the 10th year to the end of the 18th, which is another 9 year period. Likewise, all of the letter's of John's name would follow in sequence, but after the "N" period, it would not continue to the middle name, but would start over at "J". Thus, the "J" would again have an influence from the beginning of the 46th year to the end of the 54th year.

FORECASTING PER THE ASO-NEITH SYSTEM

Clement teaches that the influence of the Cycle letter must always be taken into consideration when reading a name. This is because the best or most fortunate Birth and Name vibrations may be offset to some degree by the adverse influence of a bad Cycle. For example, if John, whose name totals to a "20", which reduces to a "2", was born on the 8th, the combination is in concord, which is in general a good combination, but when he enters the "N" Cycle in his 28th year, this great combination is offset by the inharmonious influence of the "5" during the "N" Cycle, unless the letter is in some way sympathetic to the Birth Number. This concept is also demonstrated by Clement in some sample cases in his book. For example, he says that if the Birth Number is "2" and the Name is "6", though not in concord, they are both sympathetic towards each other as both hold some of the same characteristics, like sensitiveness and self-reliance, with tendencies to extremes.

As you can see, it is quite simple. The major key to being able to interpret what will take place during these periods is the degree to which one understands the influence of the letters. Thus, a thorough and detailed synopsis of every letter and how it plays in the life of the individual is essential to reading the name and the cycles in one's life. Now, we will use what we have learned to attempt to decipher more of what Gann says in the 1919 article with respect to the specific dates and years that he mentions regarding Wilhelm Hohenzollern.

With respect to the years, Gann says,

> "His sixty-first year, 1919 will prove to be the most unfortunate in his career, and I very seriously doubt if he will live to see the end of the year. He will suffer the almost complete loss of his wealth. The death of one of his sons, probably the Crown Prince, is indicated. There is also danger of imprisonment and severe illness."

Using the 9-year Cycle method described by Clement, we find that in the given name, he would be under the influence of the letter "M".

W	I	L	H	E	L	M
9	18	27	36	45	54	63

Furthermore, take note of the fact that the 61st year would be the 7th year within the "M" 9-year cycle. Under the influence of the letter "M", it has already been stated that in discord, it would bring many burdens into the life, but nothing as specific as Gann described in the article. Next, looking at the mother's maiden name, we find that he would be under the influence of the "W".

```
W   E   T   T   I   N
9   18  27  36  45  54
63
```

Once again, we have dealt with this letter in previous chapters, and while it is negative tending towards selfishness and dishonesty, there is no indication as to loss of wealth, death of any relatives, danger of imprisonment, etc. When we consider his surname, we find that he would be under the influence of the "O".

```
H   O   H   E   N   Z   O   L   L   E   R   N
9   18  27  36  45  54  63
```

The O would be a positive influence as it is in harmony with the Birth Number. Taking all of the above into consideration, the things that Gann says in the article regarding the 61st year do not match with the method of forecasting per the cycles in Clement's book. Furthermore, in the first mention of any specific favorable or unfavorable periods in the article, Gann says,

> "The numbers '5', '7', and '9' are very unfavorable for him [Wilhelm]. The fifth, seventh and ninth months of the year, as well as the fifth, seventh and ninth months from his birthday, are very evil and eventful in his life. Observe that he abdicated on his evil day, the ninth, in his evil month, November."

Right away, we can note some additional differences from what Clement tells us in his book. We know that Wilhelm was born on January 27, 1859 and that 27 reduces to a "9", which puts his Birth Number in the 3-6-9 concord. According to Clement, the 9th day of the month and 9th month of the year would be favorable for him, yet Gann says that they are very unfavorable for him. In fact, he takes it a step further and says that they are very evil.

In addition to what has been stated above, there is another difference where Gann says that the fifth, seventh, and ninth months from his birthday are evil and eventful in his life. Clement only tells us that the number of the month of the year is either harmonious or inharmonious. He doesn't count the number of months from the birthday. After trying numerous things to try to decipher how Gann came up with these numbers, none of the methods given by Clement or Aso-Neith seemed to provide a solution. I came to the conclusion that Gann was using some other method to determine unfavorable and eventful periods. I finally found the clue that I was looking for, and it was right under my nose for the longest time, but I just wasn't able to put it together. It has to do with the second component of what Gann used in his work, and this embodies the concept of periodicity.

7

Periodicity

Some time ago while doing some research, I came across a book entitled, *Periodicity: The Absolute Law of the Universe* by Jos. Rhodes Buchanan. It has a copyright date of 1897. I had this book for some time as a digital file on my laptop, but more recently when researching something, this book popped up in my search. Unaware that I already had it on my laptop, I downloaded another copy and upon perusing its contents I recalled the fact that I had seen this material before, and after a quick search on the laptop, I found the copy I had already downloaded at an earlier date.

What really stuck out to me the second time around was the words written on the cover of this digital file. It says,

> "The Science of Destiny for all Men and Nations: Demonstrated in the Scientific and Historic Law of Periodicity: A Wonderful Scientific Secret Revealed Giving Every Man a Key to His Own Life and a Revelation of Other Lives: Bonaparte the example: Applied to the History of the World and of The United States."

I now have three different hard copies of this book, and none of the covers resemble the digital file with the above words on the cover. I mention it because it sounds a lot like Gann, and that's not the only similarity between some of the things that Gann wrote, and the words of Mr. Buchanan, but more on that later.

PERIODICITY

It is worth mentioning that Gann wrote much on the concept of periodicity. In the famous *Ticker and Investment Digest* article dated December 1909, he writes,

"Since all great swings or movements of the market are cyclic they act in accordance with periodic law."

He also writes,

"In going over the history of markets and the great mass of related statistics, it soon becomes apparent that certain laws govern the changes and variations in the value of stocks and there exists a periodic or cyclic law, which is at the back of all these movements."

So what is the periodic law? In a book entitled, *On The Discovery of The Periodic Law* by John A. R. Newlands, he states,

"In an appendix to this paper (*Chemical News*, vol. x. p. 94), August 20, 1864, I announced the existence of a simple relation or law among the elements when arranged in the natural order of their atomic weights, to the effect that the eighth element, starting from a given one, was a sort of repetition of the first, or that elements belonging to the same group stood to each other in relation similar to that between the extremes of one or more octaves in music. . . In the *Chemical News*, vol. xii. pp. 83 and 94 (August 18 and 25, 1865), I published a full horizontal arrangement of the elements in order of atomic weight, and proposed to designate the simple relation existing between them by the provisional term "law of octaves." This law has since been called by M. Mendelejeff [Mendeleev] the "periodic law.""

John Newlands was an English chemist who noted that many pairs of similar elements existed which differed by some multiple of eight in mass number, and was the first person to assign them an atomic number. When his law of octaves was printed in *Chemistry News,* likening this periodicity of eights to the musical scale, it was ridiculed by some of his contemporaries. The importance of his analysis was only recognized by the Chemistry Society with a Gold Medal some five years after they recognized Mendeleev.

Dimitri Mendeleev was a Russian Chemist and inventor who is credited with formulating the periodic law. Apparently, he was unaware of previous publications regarding the law of octaves of John Newlands. Mendeleev created his own periodic table of elements, which is much like the one we use today.

Since the publication of the law of octaves by John Newlands in 1864, there are a few more publications on periodicity worth mentioning because they are related to the subject matter of this book. The first that I would like to mention is an article written by W. F. Barrett in the *Quarterly Journal of Science* dated January, 1870.

There is a section in the article where he talks about the harmony of color and music. By comparing wave lengths of light with wave-lengths of sound, not their actual lengths, but the ratio of one to the other, Barrett was able to show that they agree mathematically with respect to the septimal scale which divides them. To do this, he reduced the best determinations of color wave-lengths for his day into a common ratio, and compared the results with the wave-lenghts of the notes of the musical scale reduced to the same ratio. Below is a table reproduced from the book of the limits of wave-lengths of the different colors of the spectrum as determined by a Prof. Listing.

TABLE OF WAVE-LENGTHS OF COLOURS IN THE SPECTRUM.
WAVE-LENGTHS: IN MILLIONTHS OF A MILLIMETER

Name.	Limit.	Mean.	Ratio.
Red	723 to 647	685	100
Orange	647 to 586	616	89
Yellow	586 to 535	560	81
Green	535 to 492	513	75
Blue	492 to 455	473	69
Indigo	455 to 424	439	64
Violet	424 to 397	410	60

Following is a table reproduced from the book showing the middle notes of the musical scale along with their wave-lengths and their reduction to a common ratio, taking the note "C" as 100.

PERIODICITY

TABLE OF WAVE-LENGTHS OF NOTES OF SCALE

Name.	Wave-length in inches.	Ratio.
C	52	100
D	46 1/3	89
E	42	80
F	39	75
G	35	67
A	31	60
B	27 1/2	53
C_2	26	50

Putting the two ratios together, Barrett comes up with the following relationships:

RATIO OF WAVE-LENGTHS OF NOTES COMPARES TO RATIO OF WAVE-LENGTHS OF COLOURS.

Notes.	Ratio.	Colours.	Ratio.
C	100	Red	100
D	89	Orange	89
E	80	Yellow	81
F	75	Green	75
G	67	Blue and indigo (mean)	67
A	60	Violet	60
B	53	[Ultra Violet	53]
C_2	50	[Obscure	50]

In regards to the table above, he has this to say,

> "Assuming the note C to correspond to the colour red, then we find D exactly corresponds to orange, E to yellow, and F to green. Blue and indigo, being difficult to localize, or even distinguish in the spectrum, they are put together: their mean exactly corresponds to the note G. Violet would then exactly correspond to the ratio given by the note A."

He goes on to point out that placing two colors nearly alike next to each other is bad, just as it is well known that two adjacent notes of the scale sounded together produce discord. Selecting and sounding together two different notes may produce either discord or harmony just as with the placement of certain colors next to each other. As an example, he says that the notes D and E together are bad, just as orange and yellow when contrasted. However, C and G harmonize perfectly as do red and blue. Likewise, C and F is an excellent interval, and so is the combination of red and green.

So far we have seen evidence of a sevenfold scale in the periodic table of elements, color, and music. In the next book that I would like to discuss, L. B. Hellenbach takes it a step further in *Die Magie Der Zahlen als Grundlage aller Mannigfaltigkeit und das scheinbare Fatum* published in 1882. Translated from German it reads, *The Magic of Numbers as the Basis of all Diversity and Apparent Destiny*. Since I don't speak or read German, I set out to translate this book on my own using online text translators. I must say, this was very tedious work. Although I haven't translated the entire text, I have been able to translate what I felt were key chapters and portions of the text based on the translation of the Table of Contents and section headings.

In the second chapter, the author talks about the sevenfold periodicity in chemistry. The material in third chapter is on the sevenfold periodicity in the musical scale, and the fourth chapter is dedicated to the periodicity as evidenced in light vibrations or color. The author goes on to talk about the theory of numbers in ancient times, and then on to the number seven itself. I say that he takes it a step further because all of the content in this book is related to magic squares. A magic square is arranged so that the numbers in each row, column, and diagonal will add up to the same value. In the book, Hellenbach creates a 7 X 7 magic square of the notes of the musical scale. This magic square allows you to see relationships between the notes that are not present otherwise.

In another section of the book, he recounts how he came upon the idea to put the years of his life in a 9 X 9 Magic Square, and based on the relationship of the years, he was able to identify key periods that corresponded to key periods and events in his life. I don't want to go off subject too much so I won't go into the details. However, I will say that the year in the middle of the Magic square seemed to correspond to the apex of his life, and the diagonals running from top to bottom, and left to right accurately detailed the beginning and ending of key periods in his life. It sort of reminds you of the square charts in Gann's courses.

Also worth mentioning is the fact that Hellenbach suggested that some people may be governed by another square whose root is a number other than 9. It just so happened that his life seemed to work out well to the magic square of 9. He also has an example in the book where he uses the 9 X 9 magic square to work out the key periods and events in the life of Napoleon Bonaparte.

Last, but not least, William Fishbough has a book entitled, *The End of the Ages: with Forecasts of the Approaching Political, Social and Religious Reconstruction of America and the World*. The copy I have is published by Continental Publishing Company with a copyright date of 1898 by a Mrs. John A. Walker. There is a page in the beginning of the book where it has the date of birth and death for Mr. Fishbough, which indicates that he passed away on May 20, 1881. He writes in the opening pages that his book is a record of thoughts and discoveries that had been accumulating during a period of more than thirty years. In the first chapter Fishbough writes the following:

> "Many years ago the present author composed and published a volume [The Macrocosm and Microcosm] in which an attempt was made to show, that the number of degrees in each and every complete scale of evolution, is *seven*: that the order of their sequence is the same as the order of the seven notes of the diatonic scale in music, and the seven colors of the rainbow, with their harmonics and complementary relations; and that the whole system of creation, constructed on this plan, presents a grand series of octaves any one of which, being ascertained, would, in a general way, serve as a type and exponent of all the others, whether upon a higher or lower scale.
>
> The conception and demonstration of this grand law broke suddenly upon the writer's mind so long ago as the year 1848, in a manner and under circumstances which need not here be described. But since then, scientific men have independently discovered and demonstrated so much of this law as relates to the correspondence of *colors and musical sounds*, found respectively in the structure of the rainbow or prismatic spectrum, and in that of the musical scale."

He then goes on to reference Prof. Barrett's work of which I have already made mention. There is a wealth of information in Fishbough's book that would take us too far off subject to present the details in this work, but the main point I wanted to bring out is that Fishbough puts forth the theory that history proceeds in regular cycles in which, from first to last, there is a sevenfold series of differential parts or stages exactly answering to the seven distinctive degrees in the music and color scales.

In the first example in the book of testing his hypothesis, he explains that he could not seem to find anything that supported his theory until one day when he was looking over an old table of chronology of the American Republic. He saw what appeared to be something like a regular succession of waves or steps, so to speak, in the development of our own national history. More consideration revealed the fact that these waves or steps ran in periods of 12 years. He then proceeds to describe these 12 year periods, in which 7 of these would complete an octave of 84 years.

To each of these 7 periods he assigns a certain set of characteristics that are unique to each stage, and then commencing with the year 1776, describes each 12 year block in relationship to the set of characteristics assigned to each. It is worth mentioning that the end of the 7th twelve year period is in 1860. Prior to this year, around 1858 to 1859, the author ventured a prediction based on his research of these periods that the year 1860 would witness a change in our nation which would in some sense answer to a national death. It is well known that the presidential election of 1860 set the stage for the American Civil War. The nation was divided on the issue of slavery, and chaos & revolution reigned. These are the characteristics that he uses to describe the events corresponding to the first period of any cycle.

If you add an additional 84-year period to 1860, we come to 1944. It marks the end of the 7th period in another 84-year cycle, which would run from 1932 to 1944. This time period is also identified by Gann in his novel, *The Tunnel thru the Air*, where he says on page 83, "Another bad period for the United States will be 1940 to 1944." If you add another 84-year cycle to 1944, we come to 2016. This book has a wealth of ideas and information that I highly recommend it.

Now, getting back to the book written by Buchanan on periodicity, he tells us that after retirement from a Medical College in 1856, he was attracted by an apparent periodicity in nature in the phenomena of disease and in the different influences of week days, months and years, and even in his own affairs in the college. He further states,

> "Popular opinion fixed upon the sixth day of the week, Friday, as unlucky, and some of my experiments seemed to sustain that idea, which was expressed in the creative legend of Genesis, that God was fatigued on the sixth day and rested on the seventh, which was therefore ordered to be a day of rest.
>
> "Friday, the sixth day, was the day of the crucifixion of Jesus, and has since been regarded as hang-man's day, and used for that purpose. The wide spread opinion that Friday is an inauspicious day, would not have

been so long maintained without some foundation in nature, and the same impression as to the number thirteen must have been based on some experience."

From these observations he had worked up his theory on periodicity and put it to the test. He goes on to say,

"To make decisive tests of the law, I have been accustomed upon first meeting a stranger to tell him of the favorable and unfavorable periods of his life, and to find him astonished at the revelation of his troubles, the times of deadly sickness, financial loss, disappointments, calamities and failures in schemes that looked plausible."

Then, he goes on to say,

"The law which I have found in operation, and which my most intimate friends, in testing, have become convinced by experience that it is a law of great importance to be understood, is easily stated. It is this - that all vital operations proceed in varying course, measured by the number seven. This septimal division I expect to find in the life of every individual from youth to age, in the progress of diseases, in the history of nations, societies, enterprises, and everything that has progress and decline - in short in all life, for all life has its periods of birth growth decline and death."

Buchanan goes on to explain that an individual's life is governed by 7 periods of 7 years each, which amounts to 49 years in total. After the 49th year, the cycle repeats itself. Each of these 7 periods is given the name of a day of the week for easy identification. Thus, Sunday is the 1st period, Monday the 2nd, and so on to Saturday, which corresponds to the 7th.

In addition to the 7-year periods, each year within the 7-year period also corresponds to a day of the week. Thus, the first year is a Sunday year, the second year a Monday year, etc., so that like Gann says, there is a wheel within a wheel. A person could be in a Sunday 7-year period, but in a Tuesday year. Then, the year is also broken down into 7 monthly periods of approximately 52 days each. So this would be a wheel within a wheel within a wheel. Now, earlier in his book, I provided you with the passage where Buchanan explains that the sixth day was considered evil or unfavorable because it was the day that Jesus was crucified. So the start of the 6th period is a time to look out for things of an undesirable nature to occur.

In addition to what has been stated thus far, Buchanan provides another unique example behind the theory of the 6th period as being unfavorable. Dividing the year into 7 periods of approximately 52 days each, we find that the 6th period would begin on approximately the 260th day and end on day 312. When you consider that it takes 9 months or 40 weeks from conception to birth, which is approximately anywhere from 267 to 280 days, it falls right in the middle of the 6th period from conception. As Buchanan describes it in the book,

> "These rules show that in serious diseases the crises arrives on the 6th, 13th and 20th days - first on the 6th to the 8th day, the moon passing through one-fourth of its orbit - 2nd on the 13th to the 15th day, as she passes through half of her orbit - and third, the 20th to 22nd day, the moon passing through the end of its third quarter, having passed through 270 degrees.
>
> This illustrates the periodic law first stated in this book, discovered over thirty years ago - the fateful six in the number seven - and the fateful 270 - the number of days which brings us to separation from our mother and exposure to a period of danger."

Throughout the book, we find that the major theme is that the 6th period is the most evil. However, from the middle of the 4th period to the end of the 7th is also described as unfavorable because it corresponds to the latter half or decline of the year or day if starting the cycle at the spring equinox or sunrise.

Like Fishbough in 1898, Buchanan (1897) also provides us with examples of the application of these periods starting when the United States began as a nation on July 4th, 1776. In the cycle of 49 years, the Friday period would be from 1810 to 1817 and it is within this time frame Buchanan says that the unsatisfactory war with England called the war of 1812 came. Interestingly, another 49 year period would give us the 6th period in the next cycle from 1859 to 1866. I have already made mention of this time frame as it pertains to the presidential elections of 1860 that divided the nation over slavery and was the catalyst for the civil war. The next 49-year period gives us the 6th period in the next cycle from 1908 to 1915 corresponding to U.S. involvement in World War I.

Moving on, Buchanan applies his rules of periodicity to the life of Napoleon Bonaparte. He gives his date of birth as August 15, 1759. He breaks his up his life into good and

PERIODICITY

evil periods based on the year of his birth. The good periods are Sunday through the first half of Wednesday, and the evil are the latter half of Wednesday through Saturday periods. I will not go into the specifics of the yearly analysis, for the main point I would like to draw out is related to the division of the year of 365 days into 7 periods of approximately 52 days each. He identifies May and June as his evil months and a quick perusal of the table below will show you that the 6th Period of the Year runs from May 2 to June 23. This is how he identified the evil Months, and this is exactly how Gann identified it for Wilhelm Hohenzollern in the 1919 article.

1st	Sun	Aug 15 - Oct 6
2nd	Mon	Oct 6 - Nov 27
3rd	Tue	Nov 27 - Jan 18
4th	Wed	Jan 18 - Mar 11
5th	Thu	Mar 11 - May 2
6th	Fri	May 2 - June 23
7th	Sat	June 23 - Aug 15

Wilhelm Hohenzollern was born January 27, 1859, and referring to the table below, his evil (6th) monthly period is from October 14 of any year through December 6.

1st	Sun	Jan 27 - Mar 20
2nd	Mon	Mar 20 - May 11
3rd	Tue	May 11 - Jul 2
4th	Wed	Jul 2 - Aug 23
5th	Thu	Aug 23 - Oct 14
6th	Fri	Oct 14 - Dec 6
7th	Sat	Dec 6 - Jan 27

This encompasses all of the month of November. Gann writes in the 1919 article,

> "The numbers '5', '7', and '9' are very unfavorable for him. The fifth, seventh and ninth months of the year, as well as the fifth, seventh and ninth months from his birthday, are very evil and eventful in his life. Observe that he abdicated on his evil day, the ninth, in his evil month, November."

Like Buchanan, Gann doesn't provide us with the range, but he gives us the pertinent months or month that the 6th period covers. In fact, November 9, is the exact mathematical center of the 6th period for Wilhelm Hohenzollern. This is how Gann identified the 9th month and day as evil. However, to explain the references to the 5th & 7th as also being eventful, I will leave that for later in the book as I would like to continue with this theme.

There is another passage in the 1919 Gann article where Gann lists a series of dates indicating that they would be Wilhelm's most evil periods for the year. They were March 20 to 27, May 10 to 14, July 2 to 5, August 23 to 25, October 10 to 13 and November 7 to 13. If you refer back to the table on the previous page where I divided the year into 7 periods based on the Wilhelm's day of birth, you will notice that the dates identified are the same. March 20 begins his 2nd period, May 10 his third, July 2 begins his fourth period, August 23 his fifth, and October 10 to 13 would correspond to the end of the 5th and beginning of the 6th. It is now obvious that Gann is dividing the year into 7 periods to identify these key periods. The question that remains is why these are all considered evil. This will need further research to clarify.

In addition to what I found above, there is a passage in Buchanan's book that closely matches a passage in the 1919 Gann article. In the article, Gann opens the analysis by saying,

> "Wilhelm Hohenzollern, the famous imperial scoundrel, whose crimes against women and children have debauched and shocked the civilized world and caused him to be the most hated and despised man in history, was born January 27, 1859."

Now, consider what Mr. Buchanan writes on page 124 of his book concerning Napoleon Bonaparte.

> "But I must select one famous example, in the life of that imperial scoundrel, Napoleon Bonaparte, whose crimes have debauched the world's conscience so completely that he still receives a tribute of admiration."

This, written in 1897, appears to be modeled by Gann to use in the opening of his analysis of the German Kaiser Wilhelm Hohenzollern in the 1919 article. They are essentially the same. Gann obviously read and studied Buchanan's book, and there is more evidence to this claim.

On page 132 of *Periodicity*, in regards to his analysis of Napoleon Bonaparte, Buchanan writes,

> "Blind to his real condition he rose again in March 1815, widely detested and met his fate at Waterloo, abdicating in his fatal month June, surrendering to England in July and imprisoned at St. Helena, dying in his evil month May 5, 1821, going to a world not entirely congenial to his nature."

In the 1919 article, Gann makes a statement that appears to be in reference to this passage by Buchanan when he writes,

> "Had the former Kaiser understood the science of letters and numbers he would have realized that he would meet his Waterloo through Woodrow Wilson, whose name stands for justice and liberty."

This passage is obviously in reference to how Napoleon met his fate at Waterloo as indicated by Buchanan. As stated before, Gann's ideas on cycles are in concord with the teachings in this book. Furthermore, with all that has been presented so far, we see why Gann thought so highly of the Bible, its chronology, and its cyclical periods.

In addition to what has been presented thus far, Gann makes a number of additional statements regarding future dates in the article. For example, right before he gives the evil periods for the year 1919, he states,

> "His sixty-first year, 1919, will prove to be the most unfortunate in his career, and I very seriously doubt if he will live to see the end of the year. He will suffer the almost complete loss of his wealth. The death of one of his sons, probably the Crown Prince, is indicated. There is also danger of imprisonment and severe illness."

As you can see, there are a number of specific statements that Gann makes with reference to the year 1919. I believe that the reason why Gann can make predictions as to what exactly he thinks will occur is through the letters of his name and the characteristics of the letters involved. However, in order to see how the letters are involved, we can take our clue from his courses where he describes the use of what he calls a Name Chart or Permanent Chart. It is the closest example outside of this article as to how Gann analyzed names.

W.D. GANN: DIVINATION BY MATHEMATICS

In the course, he describes the New York Stock Exchange permanent chart as a square of 20. That is, 20 squares up, and 20 squares over, which makes a total of 400 squares. He says that each of these squares can be used to measure days, weeks, months or years and to determine when tops and bottoms will be made against strong angles as indicated on the chart. An example of this chart is shown below.

N	E	W	Y	O	R	K	S	T	O	C	K	E	X	C	H	A	N	G	E
1812	1832	1852	1872	1892	1912	1932	1952	1972	1992	2012	2032	2052	2072	2092	2112	2132	2152	2172	2192
1811	1831	1851	1871	1891	1911	1931	1951	1971	1991	2011	2031	2051	2071	2091	2111	2131	2151	2171	2191
1810	1830	1850	1870	1890	1910	1930	1950	1970	1990	2010	2030	2050	2070	2090	2110	2130	2150	2170	2190
1809	1829	1849	1869	1889	1909	1929	1949	1969	1989	2009	2029	2049	2069	2089	2109	2129	2149	2169	2189
1808	1828	1848	1868	1888	1908	1928	1948	1968	1988	2008	2028	2048	2068	2088	2108	2128	2148	2168	2188
1807	1827	1847	1867	1887	1907	1927	1947	1967	1987	2007	2027	2047	2067	2087	2107	2127	2147	2167	2187
1806	1826	1846	1866	1886	1906	1926	1946	1966	1986	2006	2026	2046	2066	2086	2106	2126	2146	2166	2186
1805	1825	1845	1865	1885	1905	1925	1945	1965	1985	2005	2025	2045	2065	2085	2105	2125	2145	2165	2185
1804	1824	1844	1864	1884	1904	1924	1944	1964	1984	2004	2024	2044	2064	2084	2104	2124	2144	2164	2184
1803	1823	1843	1863	1883	1903	1923	1943	1963	1983	2003	2023	2043	2063	2083	2103	2123	2143	2163	2183
1802	1822	1842	1862	1882	1902	1922	1942	1962	1982	2002	2022	2042	2062	2082	2102	2122	2142	2162	2182
1801	1821	1841	1861	1881	1901	1921	1941	1961	1981	2001	2021	2041	2061	2081	2101	2121	2141	2161	2181
1800	1820	1840	1860	1880	1900	1920	1940	1960	1980	2000	2020	2040	2060	2080	2100	2120	2140	2160	2180
1799	1819	1839	1859	1879	1899	1919	1939	1959	1979	1999	2019	2039	2059	2079	2099	2119	2139	2159	2179
1798	1818	1838	1858	1878	1898	1918	1938	1958	1978	1998	2018	2038	2058	2078	2098	2118	2138	2158	2178
1797	1817	1837	1857	1877	1897	1917	1937	1957	1977	1997	2017	2037	2057	2077	2097	2117	2137	2157	2177
1796	1816	1836	1856	1876	1896	1916	1936	1956	1976	1996	2016	2036	2056	2076	2096	2116	2136	2156	2176
1795	1815	1835	1855	1875	1895	1915	1935	1955	1975	1995	2015	2035	2055	2075	2095	2115	2135	2155	2175
1794	1814	1834	1854	1874	1894	1914	1934	1954	1974	1994	2014	2034	2054	2074	2094	2114	2134	2154	2174
1793	1813	1833	1853	1873	1893	1913	1933	1953	1973	1993	2013	2033	2053	2073	2093	2113	2133	2153	2173

PERIODICITY

The New York Stock Exchange (NYSE) was incorporated on May 17, 1792. Therefore, if using the square to count the years, 1792 would begin at "0" and 1793 would end on "1", which is the first square located in the bottom left corner. It goes up 20 spaces and then starts over at the bottom in the next column and moves up again. Gann points out that 1812, 1832, 1852, 1872, 1892, 1912, and 1932 all come out on multiples of 20 years. Then he makes the following statement,

> "Note that 140, or 7 times 20, in 1932 is equal to 90° angle and is at the top of the 7th zone or the 7th space over, which indicated that 1932 was the ending of a bear campaign and great cycle and the starting of a bull market."

There are a couple of things to note here. As we learned in William Fishbough's book, he found that 7 periods of 12-year cycles seemed to characterize the evolution of the United States starting in July 1776. In this example, the NYSE is made up of 20 letters, and when we square the name, each letter in the name corresponds to a 20-year period. According to the periodic law, we should expect that there would be 7 distinct stages of 20 years each starting from its incorporation. Gann is calling this 140 years a great cycle.

Gann then tells us to look at the numbers that divide the square into equal parts, which are the years running from left to right on the NYSE starting in 1802, 1822, 1842, 1862, etc. Gann points out specifically that when the Civil War broke out, it was on the 69th square from 1792, which corresponds to the year 1861. This is on a 45 degree angle. There are additional angles that can be placed on the chart dividing the square into smaller squares. More importantly, he tell us that if we study the weeks, months, as well as the years, and apply the important points and angles, we will be able to see how they have determined the important tops and bottoms in past bull or bear campaigns.

In addition to the 20 X 20 square for the NYSE, he specifically calls the chart for United States Steel a "Name Chart". It is a 17 X 17 Square, which is also based on the number of letters in the name. In this example, the numbers making up the square are used to measure price. As such, these squares can be used to measure both price and time when it comes to stocks. The last example in these courses is what he calls the United States Permanent Master Chart, which is a 7 X 7 square based on the number of letters in the name America. He starts this chart using October 12, 1492 as the origin. He says that when you put on the years you will notice the panic years in the United States and the years of prosperity. He also adds that you can make up a Square of 21 X 21, which is the number of letters in the name, "United States of America". He con-

83

cludes the description of these Permanent or Name Charts by saying that the more you study these, you will see that numbers do determine everything in the future, and that geometrical angles and mathematical points measure every resistance level, time, price, space or volume.

Using what we know about the Permanent or Name Chart from the courses, we can analyze each of the names associated with Wilhelm in the same way. Once done, we may be able to see a bit more why Gann makes certain comments in the 1919 article. Below is the Name Chart for the given name, Wilhelm, which is a 7 X 7 square because there are seven letters in the name. Notice that after the first 49 years, you would con-

37	5 W	9 I	3 L	8 H	5 E	3 L	4 M
4 M	1866 / 7	1873 / 14	1880 / 21	1887 / 28	1894 / 35	1901 / 42	1908 / 49
3 L	1865 / 6	1872 / 13	1879 / 20	1886 / 27	1893 / 34	1900 / 41	1907 / 48
5 E	1864 / 5	1871 / 12	1878 / 19	1885 / 26	1892 / 33	1899 / 40	1906 / 47
8 H	1863 / 4	1870 / 11	1877 / 18	1884 / 25	1891 / 32	1898 / 39	1905 / 46
3 L	1862 / 3	1869 / 10	1876 / 17	1883 / 24	1890 / 31	1897 / 38	1904 / 45
9 I	1861 / 2	1868 / 9	1875 / 16	1882 / 23	1889 / 30	1896 / 37	1903 / 44
5 W	1860 / 1	1867 / 8	1874 / 15	1881 / 22	1888 / 29	1895 / 36	1902 / 43

37	5 W	9 I	3 L	8 H	5 E	3 L	4 M
4 M	1915 / 56	1922 / 63	1929 / 70	1936 / 77	1943 / 84	1950 / 91	1957 / 98
3 L	1914 / 55	1921 / 62	1928 / 69	1935 / 76	1942 / 83	1949 / 90	1956 / 97
5 E	1913 / 54	1920 / 61	1927 / 68	1934 / 75	1941 / 82	1948 / 89	1955 / 96
8 H	1912 / 53	1919 / 60	1926 / 67	1933 / 74	1940 / 81	1947 / 88	1954 / 95
3 L	1911 / 52	1918 / 59	1925 / 66	1932 / 73	1939 / 80	1946 / 87	1953 / 94
9 I	1910 / 51	1917 / 58	1924 / 65	1931 / 72	1938 / 79	1945 / 86	1952 / 93
5 W	1909 / 50	1916 / 57	1923 / 64	1930 / 71	1937 / 78	1944 / 85	1951 / 92

tinue with a new 7 X 7 square. I have only added the basic resistance angles that you would commonly see in the courses.

Wilhelm was born January 27, 1859, which would be "0", so the first square in the bottom left corner would end on 1860, which would complete the first year of life on January 27, 1860. You will notice something a little different from what you may have seen in Gann's courses, and that's the name starting from the bottom and running up along the left side. Based on the structure of the square, we can deduce that each letter at the top of each column corresponds to a 7-year period. Therefore, each letter on the left would correspond to a year within that 7-year period. For example, the first 7 year period is governed by "W", and the first year of life is also governed by "W". However, in the second year of life, which ends on January 27, 1861, the "I" would play a role within the 7-year "W" period.

PERIODICITY

Going back to the passage under investigation, Gann says that his 61st year would be the most unfortunate in his entire career and that he would doubt if Wilhelm would see the end of the year. He forecasted that he would most likely suffer the complete loss of his wealth, the death of one of his sons, possible imprisonment, and severe illness. Looking at the given name chart we find the end of the 61st year under the major 7-year cycle of the letter "I", which corresponds to the number "9". In addition, the 61st year is also under the influence of the letter "E", which corresponds to the number "5". These are two of the three numbers that Gann called evil for Wilhelm. Recall that "E" under inharmonious vibrations causes outbursts of temper, nervousness, etc., and if destructive impulses are not obeyed, all kinds of troubles follow, including nervous disorders and indigestion; loss of friends, possibly through death, but more probably through

28	5 W	5 E	2 T	2 T	9 I	5 N	28	5 W	5 E	2 T	2 T	9 I	5 N
5 N	1865 / 6	1871 / 12	1877 / 18	1883 / 24	1889 / 30	1895 / 36	5 N	1901 / 42	1907 / 48	1913 / 54	1919 / 60	1925 / 66	1931 / 72
9 I	1864 / 5	1870 / 11	1876 / 17	1882 / 23	1888 / 29	1894 / 35	9 I	1900 / 41	1906 / 47	1912 / 53	1918 / 59	1924 / 65	1930 / 71
2 T	1863 / 4	1869 / 10	1875 / 16	1881 / 22	1887 / 28	1893 / 34	2 T	1899 / 40	1905 / 46	1911 / 52	1917 / 58	1923 / 64	1929 / 70
2 T	1862 / 3	1868 / 9	1874 / 15	1880 / 21	1886 / 27	1892 / 33	2 T	1898 / 39	1904 / 45	1910 / 51	1916 / 57	1922 / 63	1928 / 69
5 E	1861 / 2	1867 / 8	1873 / 14	1879 / 20	1885 / 26	1891 / 32	5 E	1897 / 38	1903 / 44	1909 / 50	1915 / 56	1921 / 62	1927 / 68
5 W	1860 / 1	1866 / 7	1872 / 13	1878 / 19	1884 / 25	1890 / 31	5 W	1896 / 37	1902 / 43	1908 / 49	1914 / 55	1920 / 61	1926 / 67

estrangement, mishaps in business; loss of money, or similar complications.

Next, we look at his mother's maiden name, which is shown above. Notice that the 61st year is at the start of the 6-year period ruled by the letter "I". In addition, he would be under the inharmonious "W". This is another "9" "5" combination. Under the letter "I" we find that it affects the nervous direction and that extreme nervousness may develop. Knowing that the letter "E" also causes nervousness, these things are amplified starting in his 61st year. Not to mention that "W" is the Capstone for "E", so this letter provides the power to bring all of the inharmonious characteristics of the "E" to completion.

Next, we want to take a look at the surname, which contains a total of 12 letters. This requires a 12 X 12 square as shown on the following page.

W.D. GANN: DIVINATION BY MATHEMATICS

71	8 H	6 O	8 H	5 E	5 N	8 Z	6 O	3 L	3 L	5 E	9 R	5 N
5 N	1871 12	1883 24	1895 36	1907 48	1919 60	1931 72	1943 84	1955 96	1967 108	1979 120	1991 132	2003 144
9 R	1870 11	1882 23	1894 35	1906 47	1918 59	1930 71	1942 83	1954 95	1966 107	1978 119	1990 131	2002 143
5 E	1869 10	1881 22	1893 34	1905 46	1917 58	1929 70	1941 82	1953 94	1965 106	1977 118	1989 130	2001 142
3 L	1868 9	1880 21	1892 33	1904 45	1916 57	1928 69	1940 81	1952 93	1964 105	1976 117	1988 129	2000 141
3 L	1867 8	1879 20	1891 32	1903 44	1915 56	1927 68	1939 80	1951 92	1963 104	1975 116	1987 128	1999 140
6 O	1866 7	1878 19	1890 31	1902 43	1914 55	1926 67	1938 79	1950 91	1962 103	1974 115	1986 127	1998 139
8 Z	1865 6	1877 18	1889 30	1901 42	1913 54	1925 66	1937 78	1949 90	1961 102	1973 114	1985 126	1997 138
5 N	1864 5	1876 17	1888 29	1900 41	1912 53	1924<>65	1936 77	1948 89	1960 101	1972 113	1984 125	1996 137
5 E	1863 4	1875 16	1887 28	1899 40	1911 52	1923 64	1935 76	1947 88	1959 100	1971 112	1983 124	1995 136
8 H	1862 3	1874 15	1886 27	1898 39	1910 51	1922 63	1934 75	1946 87	1958 99	1970 111	1982 123	1994 135
6 O	1861 2	1873 14	1885 26	1897 38	1909 50	1921 62	1933 74	1945 86	1957 98	1969 110	1981 122	1993 134
8 H	1860 1	1872 13	1884 25	1896 37	1908 49	1920 61	1932 73	1944 85	1956 97	1968 109	1980 121	1992 133

Notice that the 61st year begins a new 12-period belonging to the letter "Z". This was also a characteristic of the Mother's maiden name which also begin a new 6-year period. In addition to the "Z", we also have the influence of the letter "H" from the left side. Both of these letters correspond to the number "8". Under the letter "Z", it says that when it is out of harmony it is not good for health. Here we find a possible reason why Gann indicates severe illness for this year. As for the letter "H", we find that in addition to developing pronounced selfishness and extreme egotism, it tends to surgical operations. We have letters that bring out similar results, and we have a combination of letters that amplify each other. Taking all of the names into consideration and the combination of

PERIODICITY

letters that are produced from the squares, I think it does offer a valid explanation as to how Gann arrived at the conclusions for Wilhelm's 61st year. Continuing with the article, Gann identifies specific periods within this year that would be key to watch for when these events would possibly take place.

> "From January 27, his birthday, until February 9, will prove to be a very unfortunate period, when he will be sick in mind and body. He will have thoughts of taking his life and may attempt it. The Allies will probably ask for his extradition.
>
> "Three critical periods are indicated:-
>
> "April 9 to May 9 will be one of the most unfavorable periods, when his life and liberty will be seriously threatened. His health will be very bad and his mind almost unbalanced. He will probably be brought to trial at this time, and if he receives the sentence it will possibly prove to be his death blow.
>
> "August will be most unfortunate. He will be much depressed from imprisonment or restraint. He will meet with opposition on every hand and reap as he has sown.
>
> "October and November are the most evil months. This third period will be most fatal and there is strong evidence that if he is still alive a violent death may take place."

As you can see, when mentioning each of the specific periods he is simply restating what he already said about the 61st year in general. There are the common elements regarding possible death, his health, mental instability, and danger of imprisonment or some kind of restraint.

The first paragraph references his birthday, January 27, and a period of 13 days ending on February 9 as a very unfortunate period. I have been unable up to this point to come up with a valid reason as to why he calculates this period to be 13 days in length or why this period would be unfavorable. However, I can offer that he references November 9 as his evil month and day when he abdicated in 1918. Thus, it is curious that he mentions February 9th as the end of the unfortunate 13-day period from his birthday. It is as if he is calculating this date from November 9th of the year. In fact, the period from November 9th to February 9th is 3 months, which is a quarter of the year. Just as he divided the year into 7 periods of approximately 52 days, he may have divided the year into 4 periods of 3 months each to find critical periods.

Consider that Gann gives Wilhelm's evil numbers as 5, 7, and 9. He says that the 5th, 7th, and 9th months of the year, as well as the 5th, 7th, and 9th months as counted from his birthday are evil. In Astrology, the square (90°) and opposition (180°) are the most evil aspects. If we apply the square angle to his birthday, we would get dates of May 27 and September 27. These are the 5th and 9th months of the year. If we apply the opposition angle to his birthday, we would get a date of July 27. This is the 7th month of the year. Could this be how Gann derived the most unfortunate numbers for an individual? If applying the square angle from November 9th, which is another important event in life of Wilhelm when he abdicated, we get February 9th. So in the last stages of this period, from January 27 to February 9th, Gann could forecast that this would be one of the most likely periods for an unfortunate event to occur.

Moving on, the remaining part of the passage under investigation cites three critical periods for the rest of the year as possibilities when these unfavorable events could take place. The first of these periods also references the 9th day of the month saying that from April 9th to May 9th would be another unfavorable period. If we apply the opposition angle to November 9th, we get May 9th as the critical date. The time leading up to May 9th would be the unfavorable period. Not surprisingly, the next period that Gann mentions is August. Applying the square angle moving back from November 9, we arrive at August 9 as the critical date. He ends the passage by referencing October and November as his evil months. The explanation for this period has already been given. He divided the year into 7 periods of 52 days and the 6th evil period from his birthday encompasses this October to November time frame.

In summary, it appears that Gann is making calculations from Wilhelm's birthday, and the date when he abdicated to make future predictions regarding the 61st year. In addition to the above, there may be another possible explanation why these periods are mentioned. Recall that the Permanent or Name Chart could be used to analyze years, months, and weeks. We have used the chart to analyze the years, but to look at the specific periods within the year, we need to look at these charts with respect to the months.

On the next page is the 15th square for the given name, but counting the months from his birthday. The first cell within the 1st square would end on February 27, 1959. The first cell within the 2nd square would end on March 27, 1963. Continuing in like manner, we find that each square of 49 cells would cover 4 years and 1 month in time. Therefore, after 12 squares the pattern of months would repeat. That is, the 13th square would repeat the same pattern of months as the 1st square. The beginning of the 13th square marks the end of the 49th and beginning of the 50th year. The 61st year would start in the 15th square on January 27, 1919 and end on January 27, 1920.

PERIODICITY

37	5 W	9 I	3 L	8 H	5 E	3 L	4 M
4 M	Oct-16 693	May-17 700	Dec-17 707	Jul-18 714	Feb-19 721	Sep-19 728	Apr-20 735
3 L	Sep-16 692	Apr-17 699	Nov-17 706	Jun-18 713	Jan-19 720	Aug-19 727	Mar-20 734
5 E	Aug-16 691	Mar-17 698	Oct-17 705	May-18 712	Dec-18 719	Jul-19 726	Feb-20 733
8 H	Jul-16 690	Feb-17 697	Sep-17 704	Apr-18 711	Nov-18 718	Jun-19 725	Jan-20 732
3 L	Jun-16 689	Jan-17 696	Aug-17 703	Mar-18 710	Oct-18 717	May-19 724	Dec-19 731
9 I	May-16 688	Dec-16 695	Jul-17 702	Feb-18 709	Sep-18 716	Apr-19 723	Nov-19 730
5 W	Apr-16 687	Nov-16 694	Jun-17 701	Jan-18 708	Aug-18 715	Mar-19 722	Oct-19 729

Looking at this square, we find that all the periods within the 61st year mentioned by Gann fall on the angles in the square. Maybe this is why Gann said that his 61st year would be most unfortunate. The first angle falls around February 4, 1919, which is in the period between January 27, 1919 and February 9, 1919 mentioned by Gann. The next set of angles fall on April 27, 1919 and May 4, 1919. These angles fall between the dates mentioned by Gann - April 9 to May 9 for the year in question. The next set up angles moving up the column would fall on August 4 and August 27, 1919. Gann says that August would be most unfortunate. The last angle falls on October 27, 1919, and Gann says that October to November would be his most evil months. Could this just be a coincidence?

We can also enumerate the months using his Mother's maiden name. A 6 X 6 square is equivalent to 36 months or 3 years. That is, the pattern of months within the square would repeat after 3 years. The end of the 20th square would complete 60 years and a new square would start the 61st year. The twelve months of the 61st year would encompass the first two columns of the 21st square, which is shown below. Although the given name is the one that sets up the vibrations in the body according to Gann, we can find additional evidence from this square to support one of the critical periods mentioned by Gann. In the square below, we can see that the April to May time frame also falls on the angles.

89

		5 W	5 E	2 T	2 T	9 I	5 N
	28						
5	N	Jul-19 726	Jan-20 732	Jul-20 738	Jan-21 744	Jul-21 750	Jan-22 756
9	I	Jun-19 725	Dec-19 731	Jun-20 737	Dec-20 743	Jun-21 749	Dec-21 755
2	T	May-19 724	Nov-19 730	May-20 736	Nov-20 742	May-21 748	Nov-21 754
2	T	Apr-19 723	Oct-19 729	Apr-20 735	Oct-20 741	Apr-21 747	Oct-21 753
5	E	Mar-19 722	Sep-19 728	Mar-20 734	Sep-20 740	Mar-21 746	Sep-21 752
5	W	Feb-19 721	Aug-19 727	Feb-20 733	Aug-20 739	Feb-21 745	Aug-21 751

To enumerate the months of the surname would require a 12 X 12 square. One square would total 144 months or 12 years. Five of these squares would complete the end of the 60th year. Thus, the 61st year would also start a new square. The entire 12 months of that year would fall into the first column under the letter "H". This is shown in the square on the following page. Here we see that July 27 and August 27 fall on the angles, which would fall into the August date mentioned by Gann as a critical period for the 61st year.

With respect to these squares, I have only attempted to provide a possible explanation as to how Gann divined the name in the 1919 article. This was based on Gann's own material regarding these squares in his courses. I make no claims that this is for sure how he did it, only that it is a possibility. As for the concept of periodicity and the periodic law, I am confident based on the evidence compiled and provided thus far, that this was an important element to how Gann forecasted future periods. In relationship to this, I find that the periodic law is a major theme running throughout Gann's novel, *The Tunnel Thru the Air*. In fact, I believe that this was the major thing that Gann veiled within the pages of this novel. In the foreword, Gann states,

"Robert Gordon's seven days will no longer be a mystery because you will have gained understanding."

PERIODICITY

71	8 H	6 O	8 H	5 E	5 N	8 Z	6 O	3 L	3 L	5 E	9 R	5 N
5 N	Jan-20 732	Jan-21 744	Jan-22 756	Jan-23 768	Jan-24 780	Jan-25 792	Jan-26 804	Jan-27 816	Jan-28 828	Jan-29 840	Jan-30 852	Jan-31 864
9 R	Dec-19 731	Dec-20 743	Dec-21 755	Dec-22 767	Dec-23 779	Dec-24 791	Dec-25 803	Dec-26 815	Dec-27 827	Dec-28 839	Dec-29 851	Dec-30 863
5 E	Nov-19 730	Nov-20 742	Nov-21 754	Nov-22 766	Nov-23 778	Nov-24 790	Nov-25 802	Nov-26 814	Nov-27 826	Nov-28 838	Nov-29 850	Nov-30 862
3 L	Oct-19 729	Oct-20 741	Oct-21 753	Oct-22 765	Oct-23 777	Oct-24 789	Oct-25 801	Oct-26 813	Oct-27 825	Oct-28 837	Oct-29 849	Oct-30 861
3 L	Sep-19 728	Sep-20 740	Sep-21 752	Sep-22 764	Sep-23 776	Sep-24 788	Sep-25 800	Sep-26 812	Sep-27 824	Sep-28 836	Sep-29 848	Sep-30 860
6 O	Aug-19 727	Aug-20 739	Aug-21 751	Aug-22 763	Aug-23 775	Aug-24 787	Aug-25 799	Aug-26 811	Aug-27 823	Aug-28 835	Aug-29 847	Aug-30 859
8 Z	Jul-19 726	Jul-20 738	Jul-21 750	Jul-22 762	Jul-23 774	Jul-24 786	Jul-25 798	Jul-26 810	Jul-27 822	Jul-28 834	Jul-29 846	Jul-30 858
5 N	Jun-19 725	Jun-20 737	Jun-21 749	Jun-22 761	Jun-23 773	Jun-24 785	Jun-25 797	Jun-26 809	Jun-27 821	Jun-28 833	Jun-29 845	Jun-30 857
5 E	May-19 724	May-20 736	May-21 748	May-22 760	May-23 772	May-24 784	May-25 796	May-26 808	May-27 820	May-28 832	May-29 844	May-30 856
8 H	Apr-19 723	Apr-20 735	Apr-21 747	Apr-22 759	Apr-23 771	Apr-24 783	Apr-25 795	Apr-26 807	Apr-27 819	Apr-28 831	Apr-29 843	Apr-30 855
6 O	Mar-19 722	Mar-20 734	Mar-21 746	Mar-22 758	Mar-23 770	Mar-24 782	Mar-25 794	Mar-26 806	Mar-27 818	Mar-28 830	Mar-29 842	Mar-30 854
8 H	Feb-19 721	Feb-20 733	Feb-21 745	Feb-22 757	Feb-23 769	Feb-24 781	Feb-25 793	Feb-26 805	Feb-27 817	Feb-28 829	Feb-29 841	Feb-30 853

Prior to this quote, Gann tells us that the Bible is the greatest books ever written and that it contains the key to the process by which you may know all there is to know. This is reiterated later in the book on page 75 where he says,

> "I hold that the Bible contains the key to the process by which man may know all there is to know of the future . . ."

In the foreword he tells us that if we follow the laws laid down in the Bible, Robert Gordon's seven days will no longer be a mystery.

So what in the Bible will help us in ascertaining the future that is also in harmony with everything else discussed thus far? It is the cycles, periodicity, and at the basis of all of this is the scale of 7. On page 370 of *Tunnel Thru the Air*, Robert Gordon goes into an explanation of how he figured the dates that he did regarding the War. He says,

> "He knew that 70 weeks indicated the end in 1932, or about 3 ½ years from the time that war first broke out in Europe in 1928."

In the Bible, the Lord had appointed a day for a year. Thus, 1 day is equal to 1 year, and 7 days is equal to 7 years. Thus, 1 week of 7 days is also equal to 7 years, and 70 weeks is equal to 490 years. This is the period of time Gann is referring to in this paragraph. We see that 490 years is composed of 7 periods of 70 years each. On page 71 with respect to Robert Gordon, it says,

> "He knew that the seventh period was always a jubilee period, that there was a jubilee period of seven years at the end of each forty-ninth year period and that there was a great period of forty-nine jubilee years at the end of seven times seventy; that the sixth period would end in 1933 and that from 1933 to 1982 would be the forty-nine years of the great jubilee following the end of wars and the United Kingdom of the World."

I believe that taking the time to understand how these time cycles work together along with the scale of 7 is the key to forecasting the future. On page 71 of *Tunnel Thru the Air*, Robert Gordon writes to Mr. Kennelworth,

> "I have figured out the repetition of each cycle when wars will come. I believe that the wheat prices forecast coming wars. Through my study of the Bible, I have determined the major and minor time factors which repeat in the history of nations, men and markets."

There is so much more to consider and look at in the novel with respect to these ideas, but this would go beyond the scope for this book and best served in another work.

8

The Secret of the Law of Vibration

In the *Milwaukee Sentinel Magazine* dated January 5, 1919, Gann says this about the Law of Vibration.

> "There is nothing to anything save and except the Law of Vibration. Vibration is fundamental, exact, universal. Nothing is exempt from it. You can watch it carefully and then own all the money in the world. You can study it for a few decades and become a prophet. You can predict events – before or after – you can become a first or second guesser just as you choose. You can even foretell what is going to be done with the man named Hohenzollern, who once was a Great War Lord and Most High Admiral of the Atlantic.
> And it is all SO simple.
> This is the secret of the Law of Vibration: -
> Find exactly by a study of geometrical angles what is meant by each letter in a man's name and his destiny is at once an open book to you. The same goes in regard to countries and rulers. That is all there is to it."

So what did Gann mean by this? We know the article is in regards to another prediction regarding the fate of Wilhelm Hohenzollern, the German Kaiser who had prior to this article, abdicated on November 9, 1918 and fled into exile in the Netherlands the next day.

Gann had previously predicted the abdication of the German Kaiser as indicated later in the article where it reads,

> "He foretold the end of the world war and the abdication of the Kaiser to the day it occurred . . . "

The article goes on to say that Mr. Gann was asked how he made his remarkable predictions regarding the Kaiser and how he determined the exact days mentioned. He wrote,

> "By the letters of his name and the name of his mother," he replied. "In this manner the future of any individual can be told. The first thing I do is get the mathematical angle, the length of the angle of his or her name and then that of the mother's name. Then you get the angle of the father's name, because that name you carry through life. Following this I take the Christian or given name, which is forced on you, so to speak, and calculate whether it is harmonious or inharmonious."

Then, later in the article Gann says that the date of birth is what determines the other angle and that this completes the circle or the square.

> "From all this data Mr. Gann calculates the "key number" which governs him [the Kaiser] through life. That "key number" is the whole secret of Mr. Gann's discovery, and this secret he keeps within himself. For instance, the "key number" of President Wilson's name is "28", and curiously enough he is the twenty-eighth President of these United States. Therefore, the numbers "2" and "8" or their total "10", will show events of importance in Mr. Wilson's career."

When Gann was divining the future for an individual he would use four components to calculate a "key number". We are told that he uses the given name, mother's maiden name, the father's name or surname, and the date of birth. In the example, the key number of President Woodrow Wilson is given as "28". What is most important to grasp is the fact that we can obtain all of the key components to calculate President Wilson's key number. This information is easily obtainable. If experimenting with methods of calculating the key number, and one of these methods yielded a key number equal to "28", then the method has the possibility of being the method used by Gann.

We know that the former President was born Thomas Woodrow Wilson, his middle name also being his mother's maiden name, and that he was born on December 28, 1856. What we don't know is what Gann meant by "length of the angle of the name". Is he simply referring to its numerical value? What about those references to finding the secret while studying ancient books on geometry and mathematics. How do they tie into the calculations? Believe me when I say, I have tried all sorts of things, but it is not my aim to show you all of what I know. In the following sections I will outline a couple of the noteworthy things I have found in my research, but only to stimulate your interests and ideas on how to calculate the key number for yourself. There is a need for more people to be doing this type of research and working along these lines.

In the third chapter I mentioned a recommended reading list from a Gann collection purchased from Ed Lambert of Lambert-Gann publishing in 1976. The online address for the location of that list is:

http://www.wdgann.com/product/W-D-Ganns-Recommended-Reading-List-21-Books

In addition to the category on numerology, there is another category listed as "Scientific and Miscellaneous". Under this category is a book entitled *The Master Key of Destiny* by Gregorius. In this book, the author introduces a system of name numerology with relationship to the Tarot. To put it in the words of the author, he writes,

> "This little book should be worth its weight in gold to every man and woman, young or old, desiring to make the most of their life and opportunities. It tells you how to accurately plan your life, when you will experience prosperity or adversity and enables you to measure the exact duration of each period of gain or loss. It tells you when to seek favors from others, when to avoid entering into new enterprises or investments, how and when to select associates, friends or employees and the best time for accomplishing your every purpose."

In the book, the author provides the reader with a list of letters and their numerical equivalents according to this system. They are much different than the so-called Pythagorean system outlined in the preceding pages of this book. It is based on number to letter assignments that are more in line with ancient Arabic, Chaldean, and Hebrew systems. The equivalent sounds in the English language are assigned their appropriate value, which is shown on the following page.

A	1	J	1	S	3
B	2	K	2	T	4
C	2	L	3	U	6
D	4	M	4	V	6
E	5	N	5	W	6
F	8	O	7	X	6
G	3	P	8	Y	1
H	8	Q	1	Z	7
I	1	R	2		

Gregorius writes on page 8,

> "According to the old rules designed for the successful application of these Arcanes to the questions and affairs of life, the position to which one may aspire is determined by means of an analysis and summing up of the strength of all the vibrations which affect and govern each individual's life."

These vibrations or components are very much similar to those used by Gann with the exception of the Mother's maiden name and the inclusion of middle names & initials. Gregorius provides us with an example by enumerating the name Warren G. Harding, and providing us with his birth date, which is given as November 2, 1865.

W	6	G	3	H	8	Birth Date
A	1			A	1	Value
R	2			R	2	November 2
R	2			D	4	Equals 8 - 11 or
E	5			I	1	8
N	5			N	5	11
				G	3	
	21		3		24	19
					6	

As you can see, the numerical values corresponding to each of the letters in the names of Mr. Harding are added to obtain a numerical value. If the resultant number is greater than 22, it is further reduced by adding the remaining digits together. This is done because there are only 22 Trumps or Arcanes in the Tarot, and each of the components is related to one of these Arcanes. The value of the birth date is derived by the use of a table that is based on the numerical value of the astrological sign corresponding to the sun's position on the day of birth, along with the corresponding degree of the sun's position in that sign. For Mr. Harding, November 2 in the year corresponds with the sun in Scorpio, which is the 8th House in Astrology and where we get the value "8", and in the 11th degree, which is where we get the value "11". These are added to obtain the value of "19".

In addition to the names and birth date, Gregorius also adds the digits within the 4-digit year to obtain another vibrational component to consider. I will not go into the additional calculations and conclusions made from all these values, but the main goal I wanted to achieve is to describe the method of calculating the so-called "vibration components".

Curious as to the origins of such a system, I began to search for systems with any similarities that were published prior to the book by Gregorius. I found evidence that as early as 1897, before Aso-Neith and Balliet, a similar system of numerology. John Hazelrigg wrote an article about this system entitled, "The Number of a Name", in the *Intelligence* in December of 1897. Although the resultant vibrational number is similarly related to the Tarot, and the numerical values assigned to the letters of the English alphabet are the same, the method of calculation is different. In Hazelrigg's article, you multiply the numerical value of the first letter by the total number of letters which form the name, and the succeeding letters successively in a decreasing ratio. Then, you add the remaining values to obtain the vibration number. As an example, this is how the name Warren would be enumerated.

```
W  6  x  6  =  36
A  1  x  5  =   5
R  2  x  4  =   8
R  2  x  3  =   6
E  5  x  2  =  10
N  5  x  1  =   5
                ──
                70
                 7
```

In addition to the article by Hazelrigg, there was another article published in 1902 entitled, "Kabalistic Astrology: The Occult Significance of a Name" in *The Metaphysical Magazine*. The author's name is not listed, but further research will show that it is none other than Sepharial or Walter Gorn Old who wrote this article. The numerical values of

W.D. GANN: DIVINATION BY MATHEMATICS

the English letters are the same, as well as the method of calculation just outlined above. In addition, the same methods employed in this article is also detailed in Sepharial's book entitled, *Your Fortune in Your Name or Kabalistic Astrology: Being the Hebraic Method of Divination by the Power of Sound, Number, and Planetary Influence.*" In this book, we also learn that the birth date is also derived in the same manner as that of Gregorius. The major difference that I would like to point out is in what Sepharial does with each of the resultant vibration numbers from each of the components being analyzed. In his book, he uses these components to calculate what he calls, a "Key Number", which is exactly the same term used by Gann in the 1919 article.

According to Sepharial, in order to calculate the key number, every digit that is part of the resultant vibration numbers is added together. As an example, using the components for Mr. Harding, the key number would be calculated as follows.

W	6	x	6	=	36		G	3	x	1	=	3		H	8	x	7	=	56		Birth Date
A	1	x	5	=	5									A	1	x	6	=	6		Value
R	2	x	4	=	8									R	2	x	5	=	10		November 2
R	2	x	3	=	6									D	4	x	4	=	16		Equals 8 - 11
E	5	x	2	=	10									I	1	x	3	=	3		
N	5	x	1	=	5									N	5	x	2	=	10		
														G	3	x	1	=	3		
					70							3							104		8 - 11

Key Number equals: 7 + 0 + 3 + 1 + 0 + 4 + 8 + 1 + 1 = 25

Notice that with Sepharial, if the vibration number is greater than 22 it is not reduced. In addition, the sign and degree of the sun are not added together either. These values are kept separate. The goal is to use the values before reduction to obtain the key number. As you can see, each of these digits is added together to obtain the key number, "25".

Now, what if we used this same method on the four components used by Gann to calculate the key number for Woodrow Wilson? This calculation is shown on the following page and you will notice that the key number doesn't match the number given by Gann in the 1919 article. I was forced to conclude that this was not the way Gann calculated the key number. I tried excluding the name "Thomas" since he did not use it later in his life, but that would cause the key number to be equal to "25".

THE SECRET OF THE LAW OF VIBRATION

T	4	x	6	=	24	W	6	x	7	=	42	W	6	x	6	=	36	Birth Date
H	8	x	5	=	40	O	7	x	6	=	42	I	1	x	5	=	5	Value
O	7	x	4	=	28	O	7	x	5	=	35	L	3	x	4	=	12	December 28
M	4	x	3	=	12	D	4	x	4	=	16	S	3	x	3	=	9	Equals 10 - 7
A	1	x	2	=	2	R	2	x	3	=	6	O	7	x	2	=	14	
S	3	x	1	=	3	O	7	x	2	=	14	N	5	x	1	=	5	
						W	6	x	1	=	6							
					109						161						81	10 - 7

Key Number equals: 1 + 9 + 1 + 6 + 1 + 8 + 1 + 1 + 7 = 35

So instead of employing the method of Hazelrigg and Sepharial, of multiplying the numerical value of the letters by the number of letters in the name in succeeding fashion, I went back to simply adding up the numerical value of the letters in the name like Gregorius. Although the addition of the digits derived from only the names will yield "28", the inclusion of all four components still does not give me the desired number as shown below.

T	4	W	6	W	6	Birth Date		
H	8	O	7	I	1	Value		
O	7	O	7	L	3	December 28		
M	4	D	4	S	3	Equals 10 - 7		
A	1	R	2	O	7			
S	3	O	7	N	5			
		W	6					
	27		39		25	10 - 7		

Key Number equals: 2 + 7 + 3 + 9 + 2 + 5 + 1 + 7 = 36

Even if I excluded the name "Thomas" from the count, the key number would be "27", which is close, but not the desired number.

Not finding any kind of success, I abandoned the Chaldean or Hebrew number to letter assignments for the Pythagorean number to letter assignments outlined earlier in the book. After all, the evidence I had pointed to Gann utilizing the system as outlined by Luo Clement. In addition, there is a passage within the 1919 article where Gann says that Woodrow's name stands for justice and liberty. Just as each letter embodies a certain set of characteristics, the numerical value of the name does as well. Although I haven't come across any material where Gann outwardly says which number to letter assignments he used, it is only when you use the Pythagorean system that Woodrow's name enumerates to "5".

```
W  O  O  D  R  O  W
5  6  6  4  9  6  5  =  41  =  5
```

This is the number corresponding to "W", and therefore, stands for justice and liberty. So in a way, Gann is telling us which number to letter system he was using. According to the system outlined by Clement, Woodrow's given name does in fact stand for justice and liberty.

Using the numerical value of Woodrow Wilson's names as calculated using the Pythagorean system, and converting his birth date to sign and degree as described by Gregorius and Sepharial, we get the following results.

						Birth Date
T	2	W	5	W	5	Value
H	8	O	6	I	9	December 28
O	6	O	6	L	3	Equals 10 - 7
M	4	D	4	S	1	
A	1	R	9	O	6	
S	1	O	6	N	5	
		W	5			
	22		41		29	10 - 7

Key Number equals: 2 + 2 + 4 + 1 + 2 + 9 + 1 + 7 = 28

Finally! The total value of these digits is "28", our desired number. Could this be the method employed by Gann to calculate the key number? Possibly, but what about the connections to geometry and geometrical figures? Only further research in connection with these concepts will prove the value of the methods employed. There is amazing information in the books that I referenced that I did not mention in this work, and there are so many more angles to explore and research in connection with this material. However, I will say no more. It is here that I will end my analysis of the 1919 article, but I hope that it is the beginning of more interest and research along these lines by individuals on the path. Peace & Blessings!

BIBLIOGRAPHY

The Aso-Neith Cryptogram. Gann Study Group. http://finance.groups.yahoo.com group/gannstudygroup/.

Balliet, L. Dow, *How to Attain Success Through the Strength of Vibration: A System of Numbers as Taught by Pythagoras*. Albuquerque: Sun Publishing Company, 1905.

Barrett, W. F., "Light and Sound: An Examination of Their Reputed Analogy." *The Quarterly Journal of Science*. Vol. VII. London: Longmans, Green, and Co., Paternoster Row. January 1870. p. 1-16.

Boyle, Veolita Parke, *The Fundamental Principles of Yi-King, Tao: The Cabbalas of Egypt and the Hebrews*. Chicago: Occult Publishing Company, 1929.

Buchanan, Jos. Rodes, *Periodicity: The Absolute Law of the Entire Universe*. Chicago: A. F. Seward & CO., 1897.

Clement, Luo, *The Ancient Science of Numbers*. New York: Rodger Brothers, 1908.

Fishbough, William, *The End of the Ages: With Forecasts of the Approaching Political, Social and Religious Reconstruction of America and the World*. New York: Continental Publishing Company, 1898.

Gregorius, *The Master Key of Destiny*. Clarewin Co., 1924.

Hazelrigg, John, "The Number of a Name." *Intelligence*. Vol. VII, No. 1. New York: The Metaphysical Publishing Company, December 1897. p. 89-92.

"Kabalistic Astrology: The Occult Significance of a Name." *The Metaphysical Magazine*. Vol. XVII, No. 2. New York: The Metaphysical Publishing Company, October-December 1902. p. 165-167.

"Free Tip." *New York Herald*. 18 April 1909: Fifth Section: Financial.

Gann, W.D., "Sees the Kaiser Shot While Trying to Flee His Prison." *The Milwaukee Sentinel Magazine*. 5 January 1919.

Gann, W.D., *The Tunnel Thru the Air Or Looking Back From 1940*. New York: Financial Guardian Publishing Co., 1927.

Gann, W.D., *The W.D. Gann Master Commodities Course*. p. 338 - 340.

Gann, W.D., *Why Money is Lost on Commodities and Stocks and How to Make Profits*. Pomeroy, WA: Lambert-Gann Publishing Company, 1954.

Hellenbach, L. B., *Die Magie Der Zahlen als Grundlage aller Mannigfaltigkeit und das scheinbare Fatum*. Wien, 1882.

"Names, Numbers and Fate." *The Sun*. 17 January 1904: p. 20.

"The Newest Way of Marrying Happily." *The Plain Dealer*. 14 March 1909: p. 52.

Newlands, John A. R., *On the Discovery of the Periodic Law, and on Relations Among the Atomic Weights*. New York: E. & F. N. Spon, 1884.

"Numbers Rule Your Fate." *The Sun*. 29 March 1903: p. 8.

Sepharial, *Your Fortune in Your Name or Kabalistic Astrology: Being the Hebraic Method of Divination by the Power of Sound, Number, and Planetary Influence*. London: Rider & Co., 1908.

"Unhappy, Your Number is Wrong." *Willmar Tribune*. 30 July 1913: p. 6.

Who Was OROLO?. Gann Study Group. http://finance.groups.yahoo.com/group gannstudygroup/.

"With the Long Bow." *The Minneapolis Journal*. 4 July, 1905: p. 12.

Wyckoff, Richard D., "William D. Gann: An Operator Whose Science and Ability Place Him in the Front Rank - His Remarkable Predictions and Trading Record." *The Ticker and Investment Digest*, Vol. 5, No. 2. December, 1909: 51-55.

Sees the Kaiser Shot While Trying to Flee His Prison

Student of the Law of Vibration, Who Also Is a Prophet of Note and a Seer of First Quality, Makes Another Prediction Regarding the Fate of the Man Named Hohenzollern, Who Until Late Said He Was the Great War Lord and Also the Most High Admiral of the Atlantic.

THERE is nothing to anything save and except the Law of Vibration. Vibration is fundamental, exact, universal. Nothing is exempt from it. You can watch it carefully and then own all the money in the world. You can study it for a few decades and become a prophet. You can predict events—before or after—you can become a first or second guesser just as you choose. You can even foretell what is going to be done with the man named Hohenzollern, who once was a Great War Lord and Most High Admiral of the Atlantic.

And it is all SO simple.

This is the secret of the Law of Vibration:—

Find exactly by a study of geometrical angles what is meant by each letter in a man's name and his destiny is at once an open book to you. The same goes in regard to countries and rulers. That is all there is to it.

Now, to explain:—

William D. Gann, a Wall street broker, is the discoverer of the Law of Vibration and its application to matters mundane. In its particular relation to the man Hohenzollern Mr. Gann wrote as follows for this Magazine:—

"Wilhelm Hohenzollern, the infamous imperial scoundrel, whose crimes against women and children have debauched and shocked the civilized world and caused him to be the most hated and despised man in history, was born January 27, 1859. His mother, Princess Victoria Adelaide Mary Louisa Wettin, was born November 21, 1840.

"A study of the mother's maiden name, which always reveals the secret nature and future destiny of the male child more than the father's name, indicates the remarkable events in the Kaiser's life. Her name shows that the husband lacked love and sympathy for her, which is fully manifested in the depraved feelings and unsympathetic nature of her son. The name Hohenzollern shows that he would inherit from his father an unbalanced mind; that he would be an egoist, a braggart and a selfish coward. No one doubts that none other than a depraved and insane mind could have conceived the idea of world dominion. No sane man would have antagonized the United States and believed he could defeat the country whose colors have never yet trailed the dust.

"His name and numbers indicated that he would inherit a throne, property and wealth and then lose them all in his own acts. His numbers reveal the fact that all vain hopes would be defeated in the end.

"The letter W is a twin letter or a letter with a dual nature. While it is one of justice and fairness, when afflicted it becomes one of the most selfish and debased influences. The letter N is the most powerful letter for producing wealth and fame, especially when the surname begins with W and ends with N. It overcomes all obstacles and wins in the end. A name ending with N leaves a record which is famous long after death, as in the case of George Washington, Abraham Lincoln, Duke of Wellington and Woodrow Wilson. When H is the initial letter, it attempts to create a position of wealth and power through destruction. It afflicts or opposes W and N. The evil tendencies Wilhelm Hohenzollern inherited from his father's name caused him to break the heart of his mother, whose noble qualities were shown by the fact that her name began with W and ended with N. Had the former Kaiser understood the science of letters and numbers he would have realized that he would meet his Waterloo through Woodrow Wilson, whose name stands for justice and liberty.

"The numbers '5,' '7' and '9' are very unfavorable for him. The fifth, seventh and ninth months of the year, as well as the fifth, seventh and ninth months from his birthday, are very evil and eventful in his life. Observe that he abdicated on his evil day, the ninth, in his evil month, November.

"His sixty-first year, 1919, will prove to be the most unfortunate in his career, and I very seriously doubt if he will live to see the end of the year. He will suffer the almost complete loss of his wealth. The death of one of his sons, probably the Crown Prince, is indicated. There is also danger of imprisonment and severe illness. The following are his most evil periods for this year:—March 20 to 27, May 10 to 14, July 2 to 5, August 23 to 25, October 10 to 13 and November 7 to 13.

"From January 27, his birthday, until February 9 will prove to be a very unfortunate period, when he will be sick in mind and body. He will have thoughts of taking his life and may attempt it. The Allies will probably ask for his extradition.

"Three critical periods are indicated:—

"April 9 to May 9 will be one of the most unfavorable periods, when his life and liberty will be seriously threatened. His health will be very bad and his mind almost unbalanced. He will probably be brought to trial at this time, and if he receives the sentence it will possibly prove to be his death blow.

"August will be most unfortunate. He will be much depressed from imprisonment or restraint. He will meet with opposition on every hand and reap as he has sown.

"October and November are the most evil months. This third period will be most fatal and there is strong evidence that if he is still alive a violent death may take place.

"His name reveals strong testimony that when brought to trial the death penalty will be inflicted, unless Woodrow Wilson intercedes in his behalf and on humane principles asks for life imprisonment, and it is strongly indicated that he will. It is a sure thing that the Kaiser will receive extreme punishment and spend the balance of his life under limitations and restraints. He will be confined either in a prison or an asylum. The end will come suddenly and not be a natural death. There is an indication that he will make an attempt to escape but in so doing will lose his life."

Mr. Gann is unknown to the general public, but his name and personality have long been familiar to Wall street. He predicted both elections of President Wilson when the judgment of keen, shrewd men favored that of his opponent. He foretold the end of the world war and the abdication of the Kaiser to the day it occurred, and his predictions regarding the movements of big stocks have been for years the talk of the brokers.

Mr. Gann is modest and unassuming and looks more like a deep student than the financier, as the public mind usually portrays him. When asked about his discovery and his predictions he tried to evade the subject at first but finally agreed to tell something about his work. He made his discovery about twenty years ago, after weeks and months of research into geometry and mathematics in ancient books and at a cost of $25,000.

He consumed eighty pounds of paper in figuring, and his geometrical deductions and calculations are contained on a roll which, when unwound, would reach from Wall street to the Battery. From all these numbers Mr. Gann erects his geometrical figures. He has a big, ponderous volume filled with these figures—squares, angles, pyramids and circles—and whenever he wants to know anything he turns to a certain geometrical figure and puts his finger on the answer.

Mr. Gann, who is a native of Texas, gave the following account of his experience and methods:—

"It is impossible now to give any adequate idea of the law of vibration as I apply it to my business; however, the layman may be able to grasp some of the principles when I state that this is the fundamental law upon which wireless telegraphy, wireless telephones, phonographs and all other great inventions are based. Without the existence of this law these inventions would have been impossible.

"In order to test my idea I have not only put in years of labor in the regular way but I spent nine months working night and day in the old Astor Library and in the British Museum, in London, poring over ancient books on mathematics and geometry as well as the records of stock transactions as far back as 1820. I have, incidentally, examined the manipulations of Jay Gould, Daniel Drew, Commodore Vanderbilt and all other important Wall street manipulators from that time to the present time.

"Vibration is fundamental; nothing is exempt from this law; it is universal, therefore applicable to every class of phenomena, animate or inanimate, on the globe."

Mr Gann added that his researches showed that the ancients had knowledge of natural laws of which we can scarcely dream; that in a sense they were wiser than we are to-day. The fact that the ancients wrote their numbers and letters in geometrical figures opened the way to his discovery of the law that rules all things. He found that every letter and every number was written in a geometrical angle that determined the power of its vibration. Knowing this vibration in the letters of an individual's name, in the letters contained in the name of a stock or in the letters of the name of a country or a ruler, the destiny of that individual, that stock or that ruler and country can be correctly seen.

"There is everything in a name or in a word," said Mr. Gann, the strong lines of his face relaxing in a genial smile, "despite all that Shakespeare has said. There is no such thing as chance in this universe, and the names which we give to our children are governed by this great law. We have all heard the story of Voltaire, who only became great and famous after he had changed his name to what we know it to-day. Perhaps he was adept in the workings of this law."

Mr. Gann was asked how he made his remarkable predictions regarding the Kaiser and how he determined the exact days mentioned.

"By the letters of his name and the name of his mother," he replied. "In this manner the fate of any individual can be told. The first thing I do is to get the mathematical angle, the length of the angle of his or her name and then that of the mother's name. Then you get the angle of the father's name, because that name you carry through life. Following this I take the Christian or given name, which is forced on you, so to speak, and calculate whether it is harmonious or inharmonious. There are just two things to everything—harmony or inharmony, positive or negative, light or darkness, beauty or ugliness. If the name given you is out of harmony then you have got to work through that until you have come into harmony. The given name gives the vibration set up in the body. Everything is based absolutely on geometry and mathematics. You have got to prove everything in a circle, in a square or in an angle. You have got to know how a pyramid stands to a circle, a circle to a square and how they all 'match up.'"

Speaking of the vibratory power of letters, Mr. Gann made out a list of the names of the Presidents of the United States. The letters W and N, he said, were the most important of all. The letter W is of a dual nature, and the ancients so indicated it in their original symbol. It is the most powerful letter according to its position in a name. It works either for justice and the loftiest ideals, or it tends to destruction and ruin. A person whose name begins with a W and terminates in an N will hold a most exalted position in life and wield great power. As an example, such a name and career was that of Washington who established the Union, and going down the whole list of Presidents that combination of letters does not occur again until we reach the name of Woodrow Wilson. The glance over the following names of Presidents will show this:—

George Washington,	James Buchanan,
John Adams,	Abraham Lincoln,
Thomas Jefferson,	Andrew Johnson,
James Madison,	U. S. Grant,
James Monroe,	R. B. Hayes,
John Q. Adams,	James A. Garfield,
Andrew Jackson,	Chester A. Arthur,
M. Van Buren,	Grover Cleveland,
Wm. H. Harrison,	Benjamin Harrison,
John Tyler,	Grover Cleveland,
James K. Polk,	William McKinley,
Z. Taylor,	Theodore Roosevelt,
Millard Fillmore,	William H. Taft,
Franklin Pierce,	Woodrow Wilson.

President Wilson's name, Mr. Gann says, is even more potent than that of Washington, for his given name also begins with a "W," and his position in the world to-day is the materialization of the great vibratory power that is inherent in these letters.

In the list of Presidents it will be noted that where the "W" does not appear the letter "N" plays an important rôle; such as for instance, the names of Jefferson, Madison, Andrew Jackson, Lincoln—which contained two "N's"—and so on.

As another striking example of the power of these letters, Mr. Gann cited that of Napoleon, whose name began with an "N" and ended with it. Here was a combination hard to beat, but he was beaten, and by none other than Wellington, the "W" and "N" combination—the beginning and the end. It must be remembered, however, that not all persons whose names may be Wilson, or Lincoln or Wellington will be equally as great. They will more or less play an important part in their various spheres, but the date of birth is what determines the other angle and also complete the circle or the square. From all this data Mr. Gann calculates the "key number" which governs him through life. That "key number" is the whole secret of Mr. Gann's discovery, and this secret he keeps within himself. For instance, the "key number of President Wilson's name is '28,' and curiously enough he is the twenty-eighth President of these United States. Therefore the numbers "2" and "8," or their total "10," will show events of importance in Mr. Wilson's career.

Another instance of a man of prominence in this country who has wielded a powerful influence is that of Henry Watterson, editor emeritus of the Louisville Courier-Journal, whose name begins with a W and terminates in an N. And so it will be seen that in all names of prominent persons in every walk of life the W and N are rarely absent, and in cases of big men where neither letter appears in the Christian or given name the key will be found in the day and year of birth.

Mr. Gann does not care much for money except to meet his daily needs, and these are simple. He made a fortune simply that he might have the leisure necessary for him to follow his ambition—to study mathematics and delve into the knowledge held by the ancients. He does not want to be regarded as a prophet or a seer, but rather as a man of science.

"An astronomer can predict to the minute when an eclipse is going to occur," he said, "but you would not consider him a prophet, would you? Of course not. He simply makes use of mathematics based on known laws of the movements of the planets in their orbits. I have found in my researches that the Chinese understood all those laws and computed the coming of eclipses thousands of years before the Egyptians and Caldeans. It is marvelous the knowledge that these ancients had. In making my predictions I use geometry and mathematics just as an astronomer does, based on immutable laws which I have discovered. There is nothing supernatural or weird about it. Some weeks ago I read an interesting article on the failure of astrologers in their predictions regarding the war.

Now there is a great deal in the vibrations of the planets, but to make accurate predictions the great law behind it all, which the ancients understood, but which they purposely refrained from putting in their books, as they wanted to keep the secret for themselves, must enter into the calculation. That is why astrology fails, for nothing can be accurate that is not based on mathematics—and so few astrologers are mathematicians.

"In March last several of my friends in Wall street asked me why I did not make a prediction on how long the war would last. I had been quite busy all along with my regular work in Wall street, and my evenings were given to calculating events for friends."

Mr. Gann here lifted a large bundle of letters from his desk. They were from men of prominence all over the country—from Governors of States, big public men in Washington and others, thanking him for his kindness in working out a geometrical figure of their lives and commenting upon his amazing accuracy.

"These are the things that keep me busy," he added, with a laugh. "But it is what I like to do; it is my play, my recreation. However I went to work on that end-of-the-war calculation, and on April 6 I sent out a typewritten statement to my friends. Well, the result is known now.

"The United States went into the war on April 6. April has always been very eventful in the history of this country. Fort Sumter was fired on in the month of April, and if you will look back over history you will find that many of the important events began or ended during the month of April. I soon found that the letters and numbers in the names of President Wilson and the Kaiser revealed some very remarkable indications. Strangely enough I found that the numbers '5,' '7' and '9' are very eventful and important in the history of this country. These same numbers are fatal numbers for Kaiser Wilhelm, and showed that his evil months this year were October and November. With all the 'N's' in his name he could not beat that powerful 'W' and 'N' combination, nor could Napoleon.

"We cannot work against the law, but we can work with the law. For instance, one of my friends came to me recently very much depressed. I found he was passing through a hard period. Health and business were affected. I again tested my discovery. I told him not to invest or speculate in any stock that was due for a rise, for he was bound to lose, but advised him to select a stock that was itself depressed and sell short. He did this and made money in a time when conditions were against him. That is what I mean by working with the law."

To Our Troops

By Mary Louise Keyes

Raise the floral arch and trellis,
Lending grace to many a space;
Hang a thousand gorgeous garlands
So they lace and interlace—
Wreaths of laurel, showers of flowers,
Greens in festoons and in loops,
All to form a peerless pathway
For the coming of "the troops."
Then with patriotic symbols
Joyous welcome manifest;
Along the line erect at shrine,
Remembering those "gone west."

Might I through some gift of magic
Breathe life into my fond dream·
Verily a golden sunset
I would fashion as the theme·
Radiant with the warmest tints
That the flaming heavens hold,
To symbolize a gratitude
That never can be told.
From our hearts profound thanksgiving
To the men who met the test:
From our souls the utmost reverence
To the souls of those "gone west."

In Preparation by the Author

W.D. GANN

DIVINATION BY MATHEMATICS: HARMONIC ANALYSIS

Made in the USA
San Bernardino, CA
29 June 2017